FINANCIAL AND BUSINESS STATEMENTS

Authored By:

Louis Rubin

Researched by the Staff of:

Wealth Achievers, Inc.

List of Advisories

Advisory 1

The Financial Statements of Corporations

1. *Financial statements are frequently not analyzed.* There are no available data concerning the number of pages which are printed each year for the purpose of giving information about the financial condition of the nation's business enterprises. The annual reports which are mailed to stockholders, the financial columns of the newspapers, the large number of daily, weekly, and monthly news sheets, and the reports upon corporations issued by the many investment services, may well bring the total to many millions. It is trite to say that while many of these reports are read, but comparatively few are digested, and some are not read at all.

It is unfortunate, but none the less true, that a vast majority of the approximately 25,000,000 holders of American corporate securities have bought these securities with little more knowledge of their worth other than the prices at which these securities were selling. Furthermore, some of those to whom has been delegated the role of management limit their interest in the statements of their companies to a mere study of the increase or decrease in the sales, and to the amount of the profit available for dividends. It is to be hoped that, during the next quarter of a century, intelligent reading of financial statements will become the rule rather than the exception.

2. *Complete analysis of statements is of recent origin.* The apathy of the stockholder, and sometimes of the management, in the interpretation of corporate reports is to some extent

explainable. Analysis of accounting data is a comparatively modern function. The use of the balance sheet as an aid to the banker in the extension of credit goes back not more than fifty years; and modern methods of analysis of statements had their inception only about twenty-five years ago. Indeed, prior to this latter date, the function of the accountant was chiefly to certify to the correctness of the entries in the books, and to discover the peculations of the embezzler. The idea that the accountant, or anyone else, can uncover flaws in the financial policy and the operation of a business by means of its statements is only beginning to be understood.

Accounting methods have developed rapidly in the last half century. With that development has come a greater need for analysis and more disposition to read financial statements intelligently. Unfortunately, the purchasers of securities, the largest group which should have a decided interest in business statements, remain in the position of having stocks and bonds sold to them usually upon recommendation only, and rarely after investigation.

The same individual who pours over the description of the mechanical advantages of an automobile, and who insists upon a road test before he decides to purchase, or who makes the most detailed examination of the construction of a house which he anticipates buying, may write his check for the purchase of shares of common stock because the name of the company appears prominently in the public prints, or because the salesman tells him it is a good "buy."

3. *The management needs financial statements.* The management of an enterprise should have paramount interest in its financial statements. It is usual, of course, for the treasurer to read carefully the statements which are brought to him by the accountants in order that he may make the necessary estimates of cash requirements to be reported to the board of directors. The sales manager certainly notes the growth of the sales and, possibly, although not always, the speed of the collections of the accounts receivable. The plant manager studies the manufacturing expenses and the inventories, and makes his plans in accordance with the results of his study.

In short, each of these officials is interested in the result of the operation of the part of the enterprise immediately under his control. The important question, however, is whether the management makes a careful over-all analysis to the end that the weak spots in the project may be strengthened. In all too many cases, the answer is no, and therein lies the cause of many financial disasters.

Complete analysis of the enterprise should show not only the strong and weak factors, but also the relation of these factors to the business as a whole. Mere departmental analysis is usually not sufficient. It may be all well and good for the sales manager to lend every effort to increase the sales, but, if the sales are increased by the accumulation of slow accounts receivable, the business does not gain thereby. The quantity of sales also has a definite relationship to the problem of invested capital, and an increase may actually result in a loss if new capital is made necessary and is costly to obtain.

4. ***Bankers are interested in financial statements.*** In addition to the investor and the management, financial statements are of importance to at least two other groups, namely, the commercial banker who is asked to extend credit to the company, and the investment banker who is asked to sell its stocks and bonds. The commercial banker is particularly interested in the immediate solvency of an enterprise, and carefully analyzes its current position. At the same time, he does not neglect the permanent values in the business, and the extent to which these values are subject to the claims of the owners and of the creditors.

The investment banker places more emphasis upon the profit-making possibilities of an enterprise than upon its immediate solvency. He is more interested in the amount of the fixed assets and the long-term liabilities, but, at the same time, he cannot ignore the current financial position. The general plan of financial analysis of an enterprise is in most respects the same for each of these groups; the emphasis however differs.

5. ***Analysis of the industry.*** A comprehensive analysis of a business enterprise may be divided into three parts. First is the analysis of the type of industry to which the company under investigation belongs. All industries are not in the same economic condition; some are young and have high hopes for a successful future, some are older and have shown little signs of change for a period of time, and some are definitely declining.

Regardless of how an industry may be classified, it is well to realize that all industries, after a long or short period, begin to decline. Popular demand for the product may start to wane, the product may become obsolete because of new inventions or new processes which have resulted in a new and better substitute, or a long period of declining earnings may eliminate all hope for a future reversal of the trend. An industry may be placed in its proper group by a study of the economic conditions under which its companies operate.

6. ***Analysis of the company.*** The second part of a comprehensive analysis deals with the individual enterprise. Regardless of the type of the industry, an individual company may show signs of strength which will place its value above that of its competitors, or it may show such signs of weakness that, regardless of how favorable the position of the industry may be, the company cannot be considered sound. To estimate the strength or weakness of the enterprise is the function of statement analysis.

7. ***Analysis of the security.*** The third part of a comprehensive analysis considers the various securities which have been issued by the company. Here is included a study of the methods by which the corporation was financed, the specifications of the contract under which the securities were issued and sold, and the safeguards which are given to the security holder. This

is security analysis which attempts to reconcile the conclusion obtained by the analysis of the company with the variations existing between this conclusion and the prices of the securities in the stock market.

It is with the second part of the complete analysis, namely, the analysis of the company, that this volume is concerned. The analytical methods described herein are limited to the analysis of statements which are prepared and issued for the use of the management, the banker, and the stockholder.

8. *Limitations upon statement analysis.* At the outset, the analyst should realize that certain factors may limit his analysis. These factors are:

    a) The incompleteness of financial data.
    b) The lack of standard terminology.
    c) The fact that accounting conventions permit variations in methods.

The problem of incomplete data is not as great today as it was a score of years ago. The regulations of the stock exchanges and the Securities and Exchange Commission have done much to help the analyst obtain complete financial data of companies which come within their jurisdictions. In addition, companies in general are now more disposed to give their stockholders information than they were formerly when a complete financial statement was assumed to offer too much information to competitors. Nevertheless, there is still a large number of companies, many local in nature, which give little or no financial information to their stockholders.

The large corporations employ skilled accountants, and their statements are the result of the most modern accounting methods. Small companies, with less resources, are more likely to have accounting systems which do not give complete data, with the result that their statements are lacking in details. The executives of such companies are also less likely to realize the necessity for analysis of the financial data. Only when adversity comes, do they realize that their management has been lacking in one of its fundamentals.

9. *The effect of competition and taxes on statements.* Income tax legislation has done much to force corporations, as well as individuals, to keep proper records. It has been said, and not without truth, that corporate balance sheets and income accounts are more exact when taxes are high than when they are low. The greater the tax, the more carefully are the operating expenses and the values of the various assets recorded.

10. *Accounting terminology and conventions.* Despite the efforts of accountants over many years to standardize the terminology of accounts, there is still lack of uniformity, particularly in the statements of industrial enterprises. The railroads, by virtue of their regulation by the Interstate Commerce Commission, have a uniform system of accounts, and the analyst can be certain that accounts of the same name in two or more railroad statements contain similar items.

He cannot make the same assumption for industrial statements where great variation exists, not only in the nomenclature, but also in the way in which the accounts are used.

Over the years, accounting rules have been standardized to some extent, but the standardization has been such as to permit a considerable amount of variation. Thus, the inclusion in operating expenses, or the exclusion from operating expenses, of certain expenditures of a non-recurring nature is permitted, and the analyst sometimes finds it necessary to adjust the profit, or the loss, because the method in use does not give the proper result.

11. *Changes in the price level not recognized in the accounts.* With the exception of the rules for valuing inventories, accounting methods do not generally recognize the loss or gain in values due to changes in the price level. While it is evident that higher prices mean that more dollars are necessary to purchase a given asset, or that a smaller amount of the same asset may be purchased with the same number of dollars, the accountant's figures are not adjusted for these phenomena.

Financial data are expressed in the number of dollars spent at the time of purchase. This figure shows the original sacrifice of the owners, and, while adjustment is made for losses due to depreciation, no recognition is usually given to the effect of changing prices. Therefore, the analyst must keep in mind that, due to changes in replacement values, the figures in the books may have to be increased or decreased for analytical purposes. In a detailed investigation, the analyst needs supplementary information concerning prices and trade customs; the company's statements do not give the complete information.

The complexity of American and Canadian industry, not only as to processes and methods of manufacturing, but also as to the financial plans of corporations, results in financial statements which are extremely complex. This complexity adds greatly to the difficulties of analysis.

In the following chapters, the main financial statements are described, and they then are separated into their component parts for analytical purposes. Methods of approach are described, and illustrations are given as to how these methods are used. It should not be supposed that every detail outlined in these chapters must be carried out by every person who wishes to analyze the statements of a company; rather it is assumed that only such tests will be chosen as seem to be the most important according to the purpose of the analysis. At the same time, the analyst must be careful to include sufficient testing to warrant a sound conclusion.

Advisory 2

The Accounting Basis for the Financial Statements

1. *Is a knowledge of accounting necessary for analysis?* Is a knowledge of accounting necessary for the analysis of financial statements? This question must be answered at the outset. If a knowledge of accounting implies a familiarity with the details of the bookkeeping process, how entries are made, how they are posted to ledgers, how controlling accounts are handled, how trial balances are taken, and all the other minutia which constitute a complete accounting system, the answer is no. At the same time, it is true that some accounting equipment is necessary for an understanding of the manner in which statements are constructed, of the source of the accounts contained therein, and the reason for these accounts.

A comprehension of the philosophy underlying the double entry system of accounting is helpful and, from that point, the greater the analyst's knowledge of accounting is, the better he is equipped for his task. Much important information concerning the financial condition of an enterprise can be obtained from its statements by one who has the fundamental principles of accounting at his command, although he may have little knowledge of the detailed rules by which the book keeper is guided. In the following pages, the basic principles of the double entry system of accounting are described. A knowledge of these principles is the minimum equipment of one who desires to study the methods of the financial analyst. Without this knowledge, many relationships in the statements would be meaningless.

2. *The double entry system.* Except for miscellaneous systems of accounts which are used by very small businesses and by individuals, the predominating system of accounting today is the double entry system. This system has been developing for almost six hundred years, and has justified itself as a satisfactory and practical means of recording the facts of the economic life of business enterprises. It is founded upon the mathematical equation; in fact, one of the first books upon the subject of the double entry system of accounting was written because its author wished to describe the arithmetical equation and used as an illustration the system of accounts then in vogue among the merchants of Venice. This was in 1494 AD. and the system was not then new. Therefore, for more than five centuries, this system of accounting has been developing. Its greatest advancement, however, has been in the last half-century. No better definition of the double entry system has been given than that written by Professor William Morse Cole twenty-five years ago in his book "The Fundamentals of Accounting." Professor Cole wrote:

"The basis of double entry is a realization that in modern business there are no assets lying around without claimants. . . . Since . . . all values are claimed by someone, it must follow that the total values . . . must equal the total claims which are established against the business by persons, including the proprietors, whose claims are recognized by it."

This is the essence of the double entry system; the fact that there is a claim against every value, and that, therefore, the total values must be equal to the total claims.

3. *Forms of values and claims.* The values in a business enterprise are known as assets, and they may be of a variety of types. Some are in the form of land and buildings, machinery and tools, furniture and fixtures; some are cash or bank deposits, or stocks and bonds; some are represented by amounts owed to the business in the form of accounts receivable, or of notes receivable; while others are stocks of materials either in the raw state, unfinished, or in the form of manufactured goods awaiting sale.

Claims exist against all these values, or assets. The claims may be of two kinds; first, the creditors, persons to whom the business is indebted. If assets are purchased on credit, values are acquired by the business, but, at the same time, liabilities are incurred. These liabilities may be merely accounts payable, open accounts, or notes payable; or they may be in the form of mortgages, bonds, or other forms of indebtedness. Each liability has a claim against the business, but its claim may or may not be against a specific asset. A mortgage, for instance, is a claim against a particular asset, real estate; but an account payable has no such claim against the inventory through the purchase of which it was incurred; it is merely a claim against values in the business as a whole, with the expectation that, as sales are made and cash is received, it will be satisfied.

The second type of claim against the values of a business is that of the owners. The ownership of a business, whether it be a single individual or fifty-thousand common stockholders, has capital invested therein. The ownership expects to be compensated, first, by a return of income, and second, by the return of its capital at some time in the future when the life of the enterprise ends. Ownership, therefore, has a claim upon the values in addition to the claims of the creditors, but it cannot be exercised until after all the claims of the creditors have been satisfied.

4. *Accounts are historical records.* The reader should realize that an accounting system, above all else, is an historical record. The events in the life of a business, from which come the need for this record, are of first importance. The accounts merely reflect these events. Business enterprises operate in an economic world, and their functions are economic; the changes which take place are economic changes, and therein lies their importance. It is of secondary importance that, after a business transaction takes place, the bookkeeper, in accordance with definite rules, debits and credits certain accounts.

The fact that the transaction has caused a shifting of values from one thing to another, or that one individual has given up his claim to another is of primary importance. Therefore, it is of consequence that the analyst be able to visualize, from the accounts and statements, the economic changes which have taken place, rather than the accounting rules in accordance with which the records were made.

5. *The accounting equation.* At the beginning of every business, there is a contribution of some kind of capital by those who engage in the business. This contribution may be $500.00 in cash which is advanced by one who wishes to sell sandwiches and ice cream cones at a seashore resort; or it may be $10,000 in cash, plus a building, which is advanced by two or more persons who wish to manufacture mousetraps; or it may be $10,000,000 paid by the purchasers of the capital stock of a corporation which is promoted for the manufacture of roofing materials. In each of these cases, the business project receives value subject to a claim of the owners. Whether the original investment is $5,000,000 or $5,000, the fundamental relationship is the same; the difference is only one of size.

The economic situation at the beginning of any business enterprise can be expressed in the form of an equation:

Values= Ownership

Assets= Capital

This equation is known as the accounting equation, and everything that happens in a business throughout its existence causes a change or changes in this equation. Assets may be acquired or sold, claimants may appear or disappear, capital may rise or fall, but the equation still remains, changed in appearance but always in equilibrium.

6. **The investment of cash in a business.** Suppose that a group of individuals join together to organize a company for the manufacture of radios. The necessary legal arrangements are made, and capital stock of $10,000,000, par value $100.00 per share, is authorized by the charter. This stock is sold and the company is ready to begin its operations. At this point, the accounting equation is as follows:

Cash $10,000,000=Capital Stock $10,000,000

The cash is value, an asset; opposed to it is the claim of the stockholders who have invested their funds in the corporation.

The board of directors authorize the purchase of a plant, paying cash amounting to $9,000,000. A shift in values thereupon takes place; the cash is reduced and a new value appears in the form of a plant. The claim of the stockholders now is partly against the cash and partly against the factory building and equipment.

7. **Purchases are made.** The company now needs raw materials with which to construct radios. Therefore, the company purchases wire, tubes, and other materials, and, instead of paying cash for them, it buys them on credit. Value has now been added to the business in the form of inventories, and, for the first time, a claim other than that of the owners appears. The enterprises which extended credit for the purchases have a claim, not upon the inventories which they sold, but upon the total assets of the business from which they expect to be paid later.

8. **Goods are sold.** The inventory is put into process and part of it is turned into radios, which are sold to customers. Some of the customers pay cash for their purchases, while credit is extended to others. Furthermore, the value received for the radios which are sold is greater than the cost of the materials which went into them. Omitting for the time being the problem of the various manufacturing costs, some of the inventory is gone, the cash is increased by the amount received from customers, value in the form of accounts receivable appears, and the ownership claim is increased because a profit is made on the transactions. Goods costing $400,000 are sold for $600,000. Cash of $300,000 is received; and $300,000 is due by customers, on account.

Reviewing the transactions to this point, it should be noticed that the following things have happened:

a) An increase of an asset (Plant) was brought about by a decrease in another asset (Cash).
b) An increase in an asset (Inventory) was brought about by an additional claim, a liability (Accounts Payable).
c) An increase of an asset (Cash) was brought about by the decrease of another asset (Inventory).
d) An increase of an asset (Accounts Receivable) resulted from the decrease of another asset (Inventory).
e) The claim of the owners (Capital Stock) increased due to the fact that a profit was made which increased the total values.

9. *Expenses are incurred.* Keeping these changes of values and claims in mind, let us proceed with several more transactions. During the process of manufacturing the radios, the payment of cash for certain manufacturing expenses, including the wages of the workers, is necessary. These expenses initially represent a loss in values which reduces the claim of the owners. The loss, however, is only temporary and is retrieved when the product is sold, because the sales price covers the expenses of manufacturing. Expenses of $100,000 are paid in cash. This results in a reduction of the tangible values. The claims of the creditors, which are immediate, are in no way affected. The owners, however, who have residual claim, find the values and therefore their claims reduced.

10. *Debts are paid.* It is now decided to reduce the amount of the accounts payable by paying some of the accounts in cash, amounting to $300,000, but, in the case of one creditor, by giving a thirty-day note for $100,000.

This transaction reduces the cash and the accounts payable, and changes the claim of one of the creditors from an account to a note. It is usual to record notes separately from open accounts because they are negotiable and have certain due dates.

11. *Several transactions occur.* Several things now happen. Finished radios, the parts of which are held in the inventory at a cost price of $100,000, are sold for $150,000; cash of $75,000 is received and the balance remains on credit; the notes payable are paid at maturity, and wages and other manufacturing expenses for a total of $40,000 are paid.

Finally, customers remit cash for their accounts amounting to $175,000, and creditors are paid $150,000 of their claims. In the last series of transactions, values are shifted from inventories and accounts receivable to cash, cash is reduced by the payment of expenses, the claim of the owners is both increased and decreased because of the profit made through sales and the expenses incurred, and the claims of creditors on notes and accounts are reduced.

12. *Classification of changes in the accounting equation.* With the exception of certain adjustments which may be made in the books, the above changes in the make-up of the accounting equation represent in every type that may take place. It is possible then to classify these changes as follows:

   a) An increase in an asset may be brought about or result from:
      1) A decrease in another asset.
      2) An increase in liability.
      3) An increase of ownership (capital).
   b) A decrease of an asset may be brought about or result from:
      1) An increase of another asset.
      2) A decrease of a liability.
      3) A decrease of ownership (capital).
   c) A decrease of a liability may be brought about or result from:
      1) An increase of another liability.
      2) A decrease of an asset.
      3) An increase of ownership (capital).
   d) An increase in the claim of the owners may be brought about or result from:
      1) An increase of an asset.
      2) A profit.
   e) A decrease in the claim of the owners may be brought about or result from:
      1) A decrease of an asset.
      2) A loss.

13. *How the classification of the changes in the accounting equation is used.* The practical value to the analyst of this code of changes in the accounting equation lies in the fact that it is thereby possible to segregate the cause or causes of the increases or decreases in the accounts in a statement into a limited number of possibilities. Thus. if a plant account shows an increase of $500,000 during a given year, the analyst immediately knows that it resulted from an increase in the owners' claim, an increase in a liability, a decrease in another asset, or a combination of these three. No other causes are possible. Therefore, he looks for an increase in the capital stock or surplus, a decrease in another asset, or an increase in a liability account, such as a mortgage. Too much emphasis cannot be placed upon the fact that an understanding of the changes in the accounting equation is necessary if sound analysis of financial statements is to be undertaken.

14. *Profits and losses are not immediately deducted from or added to the owners' claim.*
The profits and expenses were added to or deducted from the owners' claim. In practice, this is done in a different manner. A large number of additions and deductions, placed in one account, would make the preparation of a statement showing the amount of the profit or loss, and the reasons therefor, extremely difficult. More details would be necessary. Therefore, a series of accounts is used to classify all the sources of profits and expenses, or losses. These accounts, when placed in the books, result in additions to the left-hand side of the equation when they represent losses, and additions to the right-hand side of the equation when they represent profits.

Thus, a complete picture of the accounting equation at a given time shows that the left-hand side contains two classes of accounts, assets and losses; while the right-hand side of the equation shows three classes of accounts, liabilities, profits, and the claim of the owners.

15. *The equation may be separated into two parts.* If it were possible to obtain a motion picture of the accounting equation as it changes due to the operations of the business, the process of shifting values and shifting claims would be depicted hour by hour, day by day. If this were to continue from January 1 to December 31, the operation of the company for a calendar year would be recorded, and if, at the close of business on December 31, the camera were stopped, a "still" picture of the accounting equation, as it appeared at that instant, would be obtained.

The first part would show the values in the business, the liabilities incurred, and the claim of the owners in addition to the liabilities as of the last day of the year. The second part would show the profits made during the year, and the expenses incurred in making those profits. Since, however, all of the accounts in the equation are not included in the first part, it will not balance; that is, the total of the assets is not exactly equal to the total of the liabilities and the owners' claim. The same is true of the second part. But. If the difference between the profits and the losses in the second part is inserted in the first part, the sides of the equation will be equal. Thus, if the losses exceed the profits, the difference is carried to the left-hand side of the first part, but if the profits exceed the losses, the difference is carried to the right-hand side of the first part.

Here, then, are the two most important statements of a business enterprise. The first is known as a statement of assets and liabilities, or a balance sheet; the second, as a statement of profit and loss, or income account. By the separation of the contents of the accounting equation into these two statements, the analyst has the primary data for his analysis of the enterprise.

16. *Changes in the accounting equation are the basis for analysis.* Having obtained the "still" picture of the equation on December 31, suppose that the camera is started again and takes a motion picture for another year. On the last day of the year, it is again stopped and a second "still" picture is obtained. The analyst now has two pictures taken one year apart. A comparison of these two pictures enables him to determine which accounts increased during the year and which decreased. An analysis of the causes of these increases and decreases gives information concerning the operations of the company, from which the analyst is able to obtain evidence as to the merits or demerits of the enterprise. The relationships between the various units, or accounts, in the accounting equation furnishes the fundamental basis for all financial analysis.

The Interpretation of the Income Account

1. *The income account.* Throughout the fiscal year, the operations of a business enterprise continue from day to day; revenues are received, expenses are incurred, the equity of the owners rises and falls. By the end of the year, a considerable volume of data has been accumulated, and these data are finally brought together in the financial statements. Those dealing with profits and losses find their way to a summary account known as the profit and loss account. The contents of this account, arranged in formal order, is known as the Income Account, or Income Statement. This statement is important in the interpretation of the operations of a business because it shows not only the net result, profit or loss, but also the causes of such profit or loss.

The description of the income account in the following pages is that of an industrial company. Terminology differs somewhat in income accounts of railroads and public utilities, but the presentation of the various groups of income and expenses is somewhat similar in form. Income accounts of railroads and public utilities are described in later chapters.

2. *The balance sheet and the income account.* The balance sheet is constructed for the purpose of showing the assets and liabilities of a business as of a given date. The analysis of the balance sheet is of great importance, but a clear conception of the condition of a business cannot be obtained unless the income account is studied coincidentally, because the income account is a summary of the financial events, during a given period, which are responsible for the increase or decrease in the owners' equity. The balance sheet reveals the extent of the change in the owners' equity; it does not show why it has changed. If the balance sheet contains misrepresentation, it is more than likely that the basic adjustments which have caused this misrepresentation are to be found in the income account.

3. *The form of the income account.* The analyst must understand the form of the income account, the financial factors which are included in it, and what they mean. In the following pages, the construction of the income account is described; in later chapters, special methods of analysis are explained.

Regardless of the type of company, or the form of statement, the first amount to appear in the income account is the gross revenue from the operations of the business. Since the object of all enterprises is to obtain revenue, which, after the payment of expenses, will produce a profit, it is logical that the amount of "intake" be stated first. Because of the lack of standard terminology, the title given to the gross operating revenue is varied. Gross Sales is most frequently used, although Gross Income and Gross Revenue are common. Whatever the title, both a gross and net amount are usually shown.

The difference between the gross and net sales includes the discounts which are allowed to customers because of prompt payment, the return of merchandise by customers, and the allowances which are made for goods damaged or lost in transit. Unless these items are sizeable, they are likely to be omitted from the formal statement. In such a case, the income account begins with Net Sales or Net Revenue.

This method may be criticized because the statement gives no information as to the amount of the discounts taken by customers, an amount which may be of considerable importance in the analysis of the operations of the credit department. If the business of the company is one in which generous and frequent discounts are offered, a paucity of discounts, together with an abnormal amount of accounts receivable and notes receivable, indicates inefficiency in the credit department, and the possibility that sales are being made to poor risks. If the business is one in which cash discounts are not usual, the discount on sales plays a relatively unimportant part in an analysis of the business.

4. *The sales.* The sales account warrants more attention than is usually accorded to it. A comparison of the sales figures for two years shows the increase or decrease in the sales expressed in dollars. An increase in the dollar amount of sales does not necessarily mean that the business is prospering, nor that the stockholders may expect higher profits or dividends in the future. The increase may have come about through one of three causes: (a), from an increase in the quantity of the product sold, (b), from an increase of the sales price of the product, or (c), from a combination of the two. In like manner, a decrease in the dollar value of sales may be caused by a decrease in volume, a decrease in price, or a combination of the two. Indeed, it is entirely possible to have an increase of sales in dollars due to a rise in prices, and, at the same time, a considerable decrease in quantity of product sold.

In order, therefore, that the sales figure may be interpreted, it is necessary to have information concerning the level of prices for the period under investigation. Some companies, in the annual report to their stock holders, give data concerning production, prices and sales. These companies are, however, in the minority, and it is usually necessary to obtain price data from other sources. When these data are obtained, the percentage of changes of prices may be applied to the sales, and the difference between the adjusted sales figure and the previous year's sales is, by inference, the amount of change due to the increase or decrease in units sold. If the company publishes complete inventory data, these data may be analyzed in conjunction with the sales, and may give a clue as to the cause of the increase or decrease.

The sales account should include only the sales of the stock-in-trade. In no case should it contain receipts from the disposal of capital assets such as land, buildings, or stocks or bonds. The total of the sales account is the quantity which is sold multiplied by the selling prices.

5. *The cost of sales of a retail company.* The calculation of the cost of sales is important. In a retailing business, it is comparatively simple. Such a business purchases its inventory from manufacturers or wholesalers at the wholesale price, and this, plus shipping expenses and insurance, is the cost of the product available for sale. To this cost is added an amount sufficient to cover the expenses of selling and administration of the business, together with an additional amount for profit. The Gross Profit on Sales is, therefore, found by comparing the cost price with the amount which is received from sales:

Sales (15,000 units @ $1.20). $18,000

Purchase price ($15,000 units @ $1.00). 15,000

Gross Profit on Sales..........................$ 3,000

This calculation assumes that all the goods purchased were sold, which is hardly likely. It is more probable that a company would purchase a greater amount of merchandise than it would sell. The total of the purchases would, therefore, include some merchandise that was still on hand. Consequently, a deduction is necessary to find the cost of the units actually sold.

6. *The cost of sales of a manufacturing company.* The calculation of the cost of sales of a manufacturing concern is more complicated because the cost per unit of product is not a matter of one figure but a collection of several. In general, the manufacturing cost of an article is composed of three elements; the cost of the materials from which the article is fabricated, the wages paid to those who work on the processing of these materials, and manufacturing expenses, popularly known as "oven head." Manufacturing expenses include all costs of manufacturing which are not included in the first two elements. Oil, fuel, repairs, depreciation applying to the manufacturing process, and wages of foremen, watchmen and elevator operators, are examples of these expenses.

7. *The inventories.* The total of these three elements, materials, labor, and manufacturing expenses, is the cost of all the product which has been put into process. It is not likely, however, that all the materials which went into process during a given year have, at the end of that year, been turned into saleable goods; some may be in an unfinished state. Furthermore, some of the product which has been finished may not have been sold. It is necessary, therefore,

as in the foregoing illustration of the retailing company, to deduct from the cost of the total product put into process the cost of that part which has still not been finished, and the cost of the finished product which is still on hand in the storeroom or salesroom. When these deductions have been made, the resulting figure is the cost of the goods which have been sold, that is, the cost of sales.

Because inventories are usually the largest and most important figure in the cost of sales, their pricing, or their valuation, has a marked effect upon the cost of sales and, in turn, upon the profit of the business. If the inventories on hand at the end of a year, particularly the raw material inventories, are priced at a high figure, the cost of sales is reduced. This increases the profits of the period, and, since this figure becomes the inventory as of the first day of the subsequent year, the cost of sales in that year will be increased, thereby reducing the profit.

On the other hand, if the inventories are priced at a low figure, the effect will be the opposite; the current cost of sales will be inflated, and the current profits decreased. The low inventory figure will then result in a low cost of sales in the subsequent period and profits will be inflated. The method of pricing inventories is not only important because it determines the value of the inventories as they appear in the balance sheet, but also because it has a marked effect upon the distribution of profits between fiscal periods.

8. *The usual valuation of inventories.* The usual accounting rule is to price inventories at their cost value, or at the replacement price, whichever is the lower. Despite the contention that this method is conservative, it fails, under certain conditions, to prorate profits properly between fiscal periods. A severe downward adjustment in inventory values may be used to throw additional profit into a subsequent period, either for the questionable purpose of tax-avoidance, or for the equally questionable purpose of forestalling the demands of the stockholders for dividends which may rightfully be theirs.

It is assumed that the company purchased raw materials during 1950 at an average price of $1.00 per unit and that, by December 31, 1950, market prices had dropped to 70¢ per unit. It is furthermore assumed that the company was able to purchase in 1951 at a price of 90¢ per unit, and that the market price on December 31, 1951 remained at that figure.

Thus, by the simple expedient of changing the method of inventory valuation, a profit of $120,000 has been transferred from 1950 to 1951. In addition, the balance sheet for the year 1950 shows the inventory at a figure of $280,000; inventory which cost $400,000. This loss in inventory may be only temporary, and much of it may be regained in 1951. Both the methods shown above have their advantages under certain conditions, and both are used. The important thing to understand is that the analyst must be on the lookout for changes in valuation methods because of their wide implications.

9. *The normal stock method.* There is a growing insistence for the pricing of inventories at a constant figure. A method widely advocated, but not so widely used, is called the normal stock method. Here, the normal inventory is estimated and priced at a figure sufficiently low that no reduction may be necessary if future market prices fall considerably. This inventory once adopted becomes the normal, and remains the same from year to year. If the quantity of materials rises above the normal, the excess is valued either at cost, or at cost or market. Suppose that the company in the last illustration decided to adopt a normal inventory of 400,000 units at a price of 60¢.

The change from cost method of valuation to normal stock method has the same effect in 1951 as the change to the cost or market method, because the inventory has been priced at a lower figure than cost. In future years, however, there will be a minimum of inventory variation because only the amount in excess of the normal will be subject to changing prices. A few large corporations have adopted the normal stock method, but it has not yet come into wide use.

The analyst welcomes a complete statement of the cost of sales because it enables him to determine the status and results of production. Unfortunately, business in general does not share his enthusiasm for such completeness, and it is a rare income account which shows separately the inventories of raw materials, goods in process, and finished goods. Usually, the inventories are all included in one total, and there is no way of learning the break-down. To make the way of the analyst still harder, many income accounts show none of the details of the cost of sales but merely give the total figure.

10. *The operating expenses.* After the calculation of the gross profit on sales, the next step is to deduct the rest of the operating expenses. These expenses include those incurred in the operation of the sales department, in the operation of the general offices of the company, and miscellaneous expenses. The depreciation of the plant and equipment is often deducted separately along with the operating expenses.

Depreciation, however, if handled exactly, should be allocated to the costs of the various departments of the business. Thus, part should be allocated to cost of manufacturing, with the remainder being divided between the costs of the selling department and the executive office of the business. While exactness is usually commendable, the result of such allocation would be to hide the depreciation charge in the various operating expenses, and the reader of the statement would have no means of checking the amount of depreciation. Therefore, it is better to deduct it as a separate item.

A large number of income accounts can be criticized because the depreciation charge is misplaced. Depreciation is an operating expense and should be deducted from income before the net profit from operations. It is frequently placed after the net profit from operations, which causes an overstatement of that amount. Sometimes, depreciation is even listed among the fixed charges, which places it in the same category as interest on bonds and taxes. Neither of these methods are defensible because depreciation is always a cost of operation.

11. *The operating ratio.* If the operating expenses are given in some detail, information is obtainable as to the extent of the expenditures of each department of the business. Frequently, they are stated in one total, in which case only a rough analysis can be made by comparing them with the sales. This comparison is usually made in percentage form, expressing the operating expenses as a percentage of the sales. The difference between this percentage and 100% (the amount of the sales) is the proportion of the income from sales which is available for the fixed charges, taxes, and for dividends to the stockholders.

The percentage of the operating expenses to the operating income is known as the operating ratio. In calculating this ratio, care must be exercised that all operating expenses are included. If the depreciation is not included, it must be added to the expenses before the ratio is calculated.

The operating ratio varies widely in the several types of businesses. This does not mean that there is a wide variation in the percentage of profits which are returned to the stockholders. The operating ratio varies for quite a different reason; it depends on the method by which the capital of the enterprise has been obtained. An enterprise which, because of its nature, must erect an extensive and expensive plant, and purchase a wealth of equipment, needs more initial capital than one which is able to proceed with a minimum of such expenditures. It may be necessary for the former to obtain some of its capital by the sale of bonds, the interest upon which constitutes a fixed charge. Consequently, such a company must have a sufficient margin of income from sales over its operating expenses not only to pay the fixed charges, but also to give the stockholders a fair return upon their investment.

Enterprises differ, therefore, as to the extent of their demand for income to cover fixed charges and dividends. The question naturally arises as to the manner in which these demands are met. How, for instance, can a cash and carry store operate profitably with a two or three per cent margin of sales over operating expenses, whereas a public utility may need a forty per cent margin. The answer is found in the relative prices which are obtained. The industry which needs a small operating ratio (a large margin of sales over expenses) must charge prices that will give it that ratio. The public utility, being regulated by the State, is given a monopoly and is permitted by the regulatory authority to charge rates which will cover its costs of operation, its fixed charges, and a fair return to its owners. Because of the large amount of capital needed, some must be obtained by the sale of bonds which, immediately upon issuance, began to pay income to their holders.

It would be extremely difficult for a new public utility to obtain all of its capital by the sale of capital stock. This fact is recognized by the various State commissions, and allowance for fixed charges is made in establishing rates. The industrial enterprise fixes its prices at "what the traffic will bear" with due regard for competition. If competition forces down prices, the enterprise must be able to reduce its costs or cease its operations. If competition is keen, the industrial must be wary in its issuance of bonds which involve fixed charges.

12. *Analysis of the operating ratio.* In the use of the operating ratio, one word of caution is necessary. It has been held by some that the operating ratio is an exact indication of the operating efficiency of an enterprise, and that the ratio should show little change as business activity rises and falls. Thus, if the normal ratio is 80%, and sales increase by 10%, it is contended that operating expenses should rise in the same proportion; or that a 15% reduction in sales should result in approximately a 15% reduction in operating expenses. According to this theory, any increase in the ratio indicates a lack of operating efficiency, while any decrease indicates a rise in the same efficiency. This is not true because operating expenses are of two kinds, those which increase and decrease with the volume of business, and those which remain constant regardless of the amount of business.

Thus, in the case of a railroad, the amounts expended for fuel, oil, or electrical current may rise and fall in direct relation to the volume of the traffic; but, regardless of the amount of freight, or of the number of passengers carried, the cost to the railroad for ticket and traffic agents, upkeep of station properties, and terminal expenses remains constant. An increase of business, therefore, may mean a smaller proportionate increase in expenses, while a decrease in business may mean a smaller proportionate decrease in expenses. Allowance must be made for this phenomenon when the operating ratio is analyzed.

13. *Other income.* The net profit from the operations of a business represents the amount of profit which has been made from carrying on its functions in the manufacture and sale of its product. This may not be the total income of the business. It is not unlikely that a part of the invested capital may be placed in assets other than those used in production.

Working capital, for instance, may be temporarily invested in marketable securities; or part of the fixed capital may be invested in the securities of subsidiary companies; or profits may have been reinvested in assets which are not used primarily for production. In no case, should the income resulting from such investments be included in operating income; it should be added after the net profit from operations has been determined. Such income is known as other income, and its addition to the net profit from operations gives a figure which is called net profit from operations and other sources. Other income is important because it gives some indication of the manner in which the capital of the enterprise is being used. If the amount of other income is small, it likely comes from the temporary investment of excess working capital (cash not immediately needed). Some types of business are of a seasonal nature, and more working capital is needed at certain times in the fiscal year than at others. The cash not needed during the off-season may be invested in government bonds, in order that some income may be realized.

Frequently, a company procures more capital than is immediately needed, in order to take care of expansion at a later date. Such capital may be invested in long-term bonds or, on occasion, loaned to subsidiary companies. The capital stocks of these corporations may have been purchased to enlarge the scope of the business, to promote economies, or to control sources of raw materials. Since a part of the earnings of the subsidiary companies will be paid back in dividends, the other income of the parent company is likely to be a sizeable amount, and a significant proportion of its total income. In order to find the source of the other income, the balance sheet must be checked. All miscellaneous assets which are income-producing may not be in the form of securities. For instance, rentals may be received from a portion of the plant which has been leased, or royalties may have been received from patent rights.

14. *Extraordinary income.* While other income results from the investment of capital in assets which are not used in production, it does not include funds which are received because of non-recurring events such as the sale of capital assets, or a refund of income taxes previously paid. These are extraordinary profits and have no place in the accounts which make up the annual net profit. Whether they are included in the net income for the year for the purpose of misleading the stockholders, or simply because of slipshod accounting methods, they distort the statement, and it must be reconstructed before it can be satisfactorily analyzed.

15. *The fixed charges.* The fixed charges of a business usually include the interest on the bonds, and the federal and state income taxes. Real estate taxes are not included because they are operating expenses. Unfortunately, many income accounts give no clue as to the contents of the taxes account. If real estate taxes are included in the fixed charges, the operating expenses are relieved of their burden, and the profit from operations is inflated. It is possible to check the amount of taxes with a rough calculation of the tax liability upon the final net profit of the company, but this can only be approximate since all deductions in the income account may not be allowed by the government for tax purposes. Such a check, however, is sufficient to bring into relief any large addition to the taxes account.

The relationship between the interest on bonds and the net income available for fixed charges is important to both the bondholder and the stockholder. The bondholder is interested in the amount by which the income available for fixed charges exceeds the interest on the obligations, because the "coverage" is an important indication of the safety of his investment. The stockholder is likewise interested in the amount of the coverage, because upon the excess amount depends the likelihood of his receiving dividends. The management of the company has an additional interest because the prices of the company's securities in the stock market are affected, and the management must always anticipate the day when it must seek additional capital.

16. *Extraordinary profits and losses.* Following the deductions of the fixed charges, the income account contains a series of miscellaneous additions and deductions. These include extraordinary profits, extraordinary losses, and adjustments. Profits or losses from the sale of capital assets, losses from fire not covered by insurance, and losses due to strikes are here included. The analyst must be sure that the accounts included in this section are of an extraordinary nature, and that they do not belong to the regular operations of the business.

Opinions differ as to the proper handling of these items. Some authorities would place them in the calculation of net profit, others after the deduction of the fixed charges, as here stated, while still others advocate the use of the surplus account, thereby eliminating them entirely from the income account. The first seem to be preferable since a figure displayed in the income account is revealed at once, whereas a deduction from, or addition to, surplus may become hidden in that account unless a detailed analysis of it is published.

17. *Dividends.* The necessary adjustments to income having been made, the resulting balance is the amount available for dividends. The dividend, or the lack of dividend, warrants attention because the dividend rate has an important bearing upon the esteem at which the securities' market holds the capital stock. Unfortunately, Wall Street frequently estimates earnings and dividends entirely from a quantitative standpoint, and fails to consider much other important data. This accounts in part for the variations between the market prices of securities and their value as estimated by the analyst.

A study of the dividend record of the corporation gives some clue to the temperament of the board of directors, and to the probability of continued dividend payments. Some corporations are noted for their liberal dividend policies, while others declare dividends only after large amounts of profits have been set aside for future use. Whether the dividend payments are large or small, their continuance depends to a considerable extent upon the stability of the earnings of the company.

Some companies, because of the type of their business, tend to have more stable earnings than others. Thus, as a general rule, companies which manufacture necessities tend to have more stable earnings over a long period of time than those which deal in luxuries, and which are more adversely affected in times of business depression. Public utilities, which operate on a monopoly basis, under government supervision, have more stable earnings than industrials which, in a competitive field, have no such advantage.

18. *The extent of income account analysis.* The extent to which the income account is analyzed depends upon the use to which the analysis is to be put. Just as the extent of balance sheet analysis depends upon whether it is to be used for long-term or short-term investment, so the extent of income account analysis depends upon whether it is to be made preparatory to the granting of credit for a short period of time, or for the benefit of the long-term investor. It may well be that, in some cases, the analyst needs only to look at the net profit in order to determine whether it is sufficient to warrant further investigation. But the mere fact that the income account shows a deficit does not necessarily mean that it has no useful purpose for further analysis.

The analyst must determine whether the deficit is merely the result of a passing situation, or whether it indicates a downward trend which may eventually lead to insolvency. A careful study of the income account should give information which will lead to a sound premise concerning the earning ability of the enterprise, a premise, however, that must be checked by additional analytical methods. These methods are discussed in later chapters.

19. *Forms of income accounts.* Three forms of income accounts follow; a complete account, a partly condensed account, and one which is fully condensed.

Advisory 3

The Interpretation of the Balance Sheet

1. *The balance sheet.* The balance sheet is a statement of the assets and the liabilities of a business at the end of a certain day or period. The income account shows the changes which have taken place in the various; profit and loss accounts during the fiscal period. The net change in the condition of the business as shown by the income account is carried by way of the surplus account to the balance sheet. A comparison of balance sheets constructed at the end of successive fiscal periods shows, therefore, how the assets and the claims against them have changed. The reason for many of these changes, however, appear in the income account, and it is therefore necessary to study both statements simultaneously.

That which has previously been stated concerning the lack of standard terminology in the income account is also true of the balance sheet. Indeed, balance sheets deviate more from standard form than do income accounts. Only in the statements of railroads, which must keep their accounts in accordance with the uniform system prescribed by the Interstate Commerce Commission is it possible to find completely standardized statements.

2. *Forms of balance sheets.* The balance sheet may be presented in one of two forms, the "account" form or the "report" form. In the account form, the assets and liabilities are placed side by side, the assets being at the left and the liabilities at the right. In the report form, the assets are listed above the liabilities. The report form is mainly used when space is of no

consequence or when a company wishes to elaborate upon the-contents of the statement. The account form is more common but not always preferable.

3. *Classes of assets and liabilities.* Assets are classified as fixed, current, and deferred. Fixed assets are those which are relatively permanent in the business, and which are purchased with the purpose of retention for some years. Land, buildings, equipment, furniture and fixtures, and permanent investments in securities are examples of fixed assets.

Current assets are those which change currently due to the operations of the business, and which are continuously moving toward the time when they will result in the receipt of cash. Cash, accounts receivable, notes receivable, inventories, and temporary investments in stocks and bonds are examples of current assets.

Deferred assets are those the consumption of which is deferred to a subsequent period. They are expenses which have been paid in advance, the use of which will not be consummated until after the date of the balance sheet. Under this general heading are also found various accrued items which are the result of adjustments made to more properly reflect the complete financial picture. Prepaid insurance and prepaid rent are examples of the former type, and accrued interest and accrued commissions illustrate the latter.

Liabilities are classified as capital, current, and deferred. Capital liabilities include the ownership of the company, represented by the capital stock and surplus if it is a corporation; or by the capital accounts of the owners if it is a partnership or individual proprietorship.

Current liabilities are those which become due and payable within a fiscal period such as accounts payable, notes payable, taxes payable, and rent payable.

Deferred liabilities arise from receipts of cash or receivables which are earnings not of the current fiscal period but of a subsequent period; or from income which applies to more than one period, and which must be spread over a series of periods. Interest and rents collected in advance are examples of the first group; while unamortized premiums on bonds is an example of the second group.

The order in which the various groups of assets and liabilities have been described is that which may be found in some published balance sheets. However, an increasing number are being published in which the assets are listed in the order of current, deferred, and fixed; the liabilities in the order of current, deferred and capital. In the past years, the order seemed to be determined by the accountant's desire to give prominence to a particular group of assets. Thus, a balance sheet to be used for purposes of obtaining credit was constructed with the current assets and current liabilities leading, while one constructed for the purpose of giving information to the long-term investor listed the fixed assets and the capital in the most prominent place, At the present time, however, it is doubtful that such reasons govern the order of the accounts in the balance sheet; it is more likely that the whim of the accountant or that of the management rules.

4. *The reserve for depreciation.* One other important difference in form may be mentioned. Some balance sheets show the reserves for depreciation as a deduction from the various fixed assets. Thus, the Plant account is listed at its cost value, the amount of depreciation is deducted, and the net amount extended into the total column. But some balance sheets deviate from this form, and list the various fixed assets with no deduction; the reserves for depreciation being listed among the deferred liabilities on the right-hand side of the statement. Whichever way the depreciation reserves are handled, the analyst sooner or later finds it necessary to calculate and analyze the net book value of each of the fixed assets in order to determine the amount of the owner's equity therein.

5. *Valuation of fixed assets.* In order to properly interpret a balance sheet, it is necessary to have some idea of the manner in which the values of the various assets have been determined. These values, if the statement has been constructed by a reliable accountant, will generally follow a more or less fixed policy. If an unusual method of valuation is used, a note is generally appended to the balance sheet. Unless the analyst, in making his various tests, finds something that makes him believe otherwise, he assumes that the balance sheet conforms to the standard accounting pattern of valuation.

Fixed assets are valued at full cost; the losses in value due to depreciation being shown in reserve accounts listed as previously described. Full cost represents the sacrifice of the owners of the business in acquiring these assets, and, therefore, represents that portion of their investment which has been placed in long-term values. Some writers deny that the balance sheet should show the original sacrifice of the investor, or owner, and argue that it should reveal the exact values in the business as of a given date. Consequently, they advocate the valuation of fixed assets at present-day or reproduction values.

If this theory be true, then the accounts of a business should not only show reproduction values but should also take into account the ever-changing purchasing power of the dollar. The fact is that the recognition in the accounts of the constant changing of valuations would soon lead the reader of a financial statement into a maze, from which he could only with extreme difficulty find his bearings and come to a sound conclusion.

When the balance sheet gives a true account of the sacrifices of the owners and of the creditors at the time at which the assets were obtained, the analyst makes whatever allowances he wishes for reproduction values and the purchasing power of the dollar. Twenty-five or more years ago, an Englishman wrote a series of articles in which he proposed a system of accounting which would adequately show the change in the purchasing power of the dollar in its relation to the accounts of a company. His theory was beyond reproach, but his system of reserve accounts, together with parallel columns for costs and adjusted values, was too complicated for efficiency.

6. *Full cost.* What is meant by full cost? The full cost of an asset at the time of its purchase, when it is bought for cash, is a simple matter—the number of dollars paid for it determines its value. But assets may be purchased in exchange for things other than cash. They may be obtained in exchange for the capital stock of the company, or of other companies. They may even be exchanged for other property. Here, two elements enter the valuation: the value of the property bought, and the value of that which was given for the property. In such cases, the analyst may have difficulty in determining the actual value of the assets. Frequently, the matter resolves itself into an engineering problem as well as a financial one.

From the standpoint of the analyst, the test of the proper valuation of the assets is the ability of the company to earn a satisfactory return upon the amount of that valuation. If he does not consider the return satisfactory, he assumes that either the enterprise is not efficiently managed, or that it is overcapitalized. In the latter case, the solution is to write down the value of the assets and reduce the equity of the stockholders accordingly. If the enterprise is earning a satisfactory return upon the investment of the stockholders, the analyst does not worry about the valuation of the fixed assets inasmuch as he is not, under ordinary circumstances, interested in liquidation values.

7. *Valuation of the current assets.* The valuation of the current assets is the next concern. Cash, of course, offers no problem of valuation, with the possible exception of cash held in foreign currencies which is subject to fluctuations in foreign exchange.

The inventories are a more difficult problem but, fortunately, most balance sheets append a note explaining the basis of valuation. The accountant's general rule is to inventory at the cost or the market price, whichever is the lower, although other methods, one of which was previously described, may be used.

The general rule for the valuation of securities owned is cost. Usually, there is a footnote to the balance sheet giving the market value. This is preferable to the method sometimes used of valuing securities at cost or market. If the amount of the securities is large) and there is great fluctuation in their values, it may be advisable to carry the increase or the decrease in an adjustment account.

When the securities are those of subsidiary companies, the formula for valuation is cost, and usually no attention is given to their market value inasmuch as they are not subject to sale, because to sell them would result in the loss of the interest in the companies. The listing of securities of subsidiary companies is limited to those of companies the balance sheets of which are not consolidated with that of the parent company. Usually, no consolidated balance sheet is issued when less than a majority of the capital stock is owned by the parent company. Ownership of forty per cent of the common stock of a company may, for instance, give virtual control if the ownership of the stock is widely distributed, even though mathematically it is not a majority. The method of constructing a consolidated balance sheet is explained in a later chapter.

Accounts and notes receivable are valued at face value. An absolute check of this valuation can only be made if the data are at hand concerning their probable payment. The analyst does not have such data unless he is a part of the management. He must, therefore, be content with a cursory analysis of the totals and with the manner in which reserve accounts have been set up to take care of possible losses. The extent of such losses varies with the type of the business, and it is usually possible to obtain data concerning the experience of enterprises of the same type as the one under investigation.

Under ordinary circumstances, with normal credit procedures, the annual allowance for bad debts should range from two to five per cent of the total accounts receivable, although companies which sell on the installment plan set aside much larger amounts. The analyst may be handicapped because the income account may not show the allowance for bad debts as a separate item. It is frequently included among the general and administrative expenses, although, on occasion, accountants place it among the selling expenses.

Consequently, the analyst must rely upon a check of the total reserve for bad debts in the balance sheet, unless the accounts receivable account is listed at a net figure. In the latter case, the analyst has no data at his command except the net amount of accounts receivable which is hardly enough to permit him to come to a conclusion. Specific methods of testing the receivables are described in a later chapter.

8. *Valuation of deferred assets.* The deferred assets may or may not be a problem for the analyst. If the deferred items include only accruals and prepayments, and the amount is not large, no particular problem arises. But they frequently include accounts which are not only of large size but which also are of particular importance in the financial life of the enterprise.

The first of these accounts is organization expense. This represents expenditures which were made in order to place the enterprise on a going basis. If these expenditures include only the expenses of obtaining a charter, the cost of books of account and printing stock certificates, together with the attorney's fee, they will not be unduly large. But, if they include promotional expenses and engineering fees, they are likely to be of considerable size. Regardless of their size, it is not considered necessary to write them down in full in the first year of the company's existence. To do so would be undesirable because a young company needs to acquire surplus profits as early in its life as possible, not only to give it financial strength, but also to enable it to render some return to the owners within a reasonable time.

Since organization expenses are pertinent to the entire life of the company, it is entirely reasonable that they be deducted from the income over a period of years. If the organization expenses appear to be entirely out of proportion to the capital of the company, the analyst may have reason to suspect that the corporation was organized for the purpose of making a profit for the promoter rather than for the stockholders. Such a corporation will likely show weaknesses when other tests are made.

9. *Discounts on treasury stock and bonds.* A second type of deferred asset which should be closely examined is that of discounts on securities, mainly on treasury stock and bonds. When bonds are sold at a discount, the corporation obligates itself to pay the full face value at maturity, but collects in cash only a portion of that amount. The difference between the cash received and the total liability must be reserved from the profits during the life of the bonds so that, theoretically at least, there will be enough value among the general assets of the company to pay the principal at maturity. If a company has not amortized its discount on bonds year by year, the profits have been overstated, and the analyst will take this into account in his estimate of the company.

Discount on treasury stock arises in a different manner. The term treasury stock is used advisedly because corporation laws do not permit capital stock to be issued as full paid unless the full value has been received. Therefore, no discount on capital stock can arise at the time of its original issue. Capital stock originally issued at a discount is really partly paid stock, and the stockholder is liable to the corporation for the difference between what he has paid and the par value of his shares.

Discount on treasury stock frequently arises from a train of circumstances which may result in an inflation of the values of the fixed assets. An explanation of this is necessary. A corporation Which has been doing business for years and has a satisfactory financial history, usually finds little difficulty in obtaining capital through the sale of capital stock. The investment bankers and the public in turn will pay good prices for such shares.

On the other hand, the infant corporation, which has nothing but anticipated earnings, may have difficulty in marketing its stock unless it can offer some inducement. One method is to sell the stock for something less than its par value, thereby causing the purchaser to feel that he is getting a bargain. But this cannot legally be done and, at the same time, make the shares full-paid and non-assessable. Investors are not interested in stock upon which they may have a liability for future payment. Capital stock can be issued full-paid and non-assessable only when it is issued in exchange for cash, for property, or for services up to the full amount of the par value.

10. *How par value capital stock is sold at a discount.* In order to permit stock to be sold at an amount below par value and, at the same time, be non-assessable, corporations sometimes

resort to a subterfuge. The promoters of the company, in accordance with a prearranged plan of organization, turn over to the company property which they have previously bought, and they receive in payment an amount of cash plus capital stock. The total of the cash and the capital stock being in excess of the value at which the property was held by its former owners, this excess is paid to the promoters presumably for their services in organizing the corporation. The promoters have arranged matters so that they are actually fully paid for their work by the amount of the cash, the capital stock being in the nature of a bonus. Since this stock was issued for property and services, it is full-paid and non-assessable.

The promoters then donate the capital stock to the corporation, which promptly places it on the books as an asset under the caption of treasury stock, and offsets the account with a credit to capital surplus. The treasury stock can now be sold for anything which it will bring, and the difference between the cash received and its book value is charged to discount on treasury stock. This account is found in the balance sheet among the deferred assets, and should be written off against income over a series of years.

Unfortunately, the usual result of such financing is to inflate the value of the fixed assets, and the discount on treasury stock may be written off against the capital surplus, in which case both disappear, leaving no clue to their existence. The inflation of assets, however, remains to plague the company in the future. To assist in eliminating the evils of this practice, laws were passed by the various States authorizing the issuance of capital stock with no par value. Such stock can be sold for any price without recourse to the foregoing subterfuge. This type of stock is discussed later in this chapter.

11. *Good will and its valuation.* The third deferred asset of more than the ordinary importance is good will. This account is a problem to the analyst because it arises in so many ways and is valued by so many different methods. Some analysts advocate the elimination of all intangibles, but there are many occasions when good will and its sister accounts, trademarks and patents, cannot be entirely disregarded.

Good will, in the legal sense, may be briefly defined as value arising from recurring profits. The courts have based their modern definitions upon one laid down by Lord Eldon in England, over two hundred years ago, in which he stated that good will was "nothing more than the probability that old customers would resort to the same place." More modern definitions describe good will as that which arises from the use of trade marks, advertising, and recurring and increasing profits.

In correct accounting and financial procedure, good will is stated in the balance sheet of a company only when it has arisen from purchase or other transaction, A company does not increase good will on its books annually because it believes that it is becoming more esteemed by the public. Under certain conditions, it may be proper to capitalize the costs of scientific research which have resulted in the discovery of a valuable process or formula, but the careful company charges these expenses against income as they occur, thereby avoiding inflation of values.

When one company purchases the assets of another company, good will may be included in the purchase price; in which case, the purchase price will be greater than the book value of the assets minus the liabilities. In such a case, good will appears among the assets in the balance sheet where it frequently remains as a deferred asset. It may be charged off gradually against income over a period of years, although some companies allow it to remain on the books until such time as their surplus accounts become large enough to absorb the entire amount.

There are several methods of calculating the value of good will. In one method, the net profits for a period of years, usually five or ten, are averaged. The average profits are then multiplied by a figure which is known as the "number of years purchase." This, theoretically, is the number of years during which the present satisfactory profits may be expected to continue by virtue of the past reputation of the company. In practice, however, the "number of years purchase" depends upon "what the traffic will bear," or upon the opinion of the court if the valuation is a result of legal proceedings. The "number of years purchase" may be as low as a number of months or it may be as high as ten years. It is a highly arbitrary factor.

Good will may also be valued by another method in which it is based on excess or super profits. Again, the average earnings for a period of years is calculated. The average is then compared with the average earnings of a number of other enterprises of substantially similar character. The amount of profits over the normal is then capitalized at a fair percentage. The resulting figure is the good will.

12. *The liabilities.* Turning to the liability side of the balance sheet, it is apparent that one great difference between the assets and the liabilities is the fact that while there may be questions concerning the valuation of the assets, there can be no doubt as to the valuation of the liabilities; their amounts are fixed and determinable. Only the possibility that all of the liabilities may not appear causes the analyst concern. His concern is justified because the omission of liabilities may change the entire financial aspect of the company. Such omission not only makes the assets appear to be unencumbered when they are not, but the equity of the owners is also overstated.

Contingent liabilities do not always appear in the balance sheet. These liabilities result from legal situations in which the company becomes obligated to pay in case others fail to do so. The amount of the contingent liability frequently appears as a footnote to the balance sheet.

13. *Notes receivable discounted.* The most frequent contingent liability is that upon notes receivable which have been discounted. If notes receivable have been obtained from customers,

they may be discounted at a bank. Upon the payment of a discount charge, the bank will advance cash for the notes and collect from the makers when the notes become due. Upon such notes, the maker is primarily liable, but in case he does not pay, the holder of the note can collect from any endorser. Thus, after the notes have been discounted, each endorser is liable if the maker does not pay at maturity. Another example of a contingent liability is that which arises when a company guarantees the dividends, or the principal and interest, of another company's securities.

14. *Secured and unsecured liabilities.* The security of, or pledges to, the liabilities are important because upon them depend the amount and type of assets that remain free to satisfy the unsecured creditors. Some liabilities are wholly secured, such as bonds which have a mortgage claim against the plant, or which are secured by stocks and bonds that are pledged as collateral. Other liabilities are partly secured, that is the amount of the assets pledged is not equal to 100% of their claims. Finally, there are unsecured liabilities, such as the an counts and notes payable, and bonds of the debenture or income type. Only after all these classes of creditors have been satisfied, do the stockholders have the right to that which remains. A study of the various claims of the creditors shows the stockholder what he may expect in the event of liquidation.

15. *Capitalization of the corporation.* The capitalization of a corporation includes the capital stock, the earned and capital surplus, and the bonds if such have been issued. The term capitalization, therefore, includes not only the equity of the owners but also capital which has been borrowed. The capital stock account represents the investment of the owners in the company; the earned surplus represents profits which have not been distributed. Capital surplus arises from such a thing as an adjustment made in the records for the revaluation of assets; it is not available for distribution in dividends. In the case of a parent-subsidiary company relationship, it arises through the purchase of capital stock of a subsidiary company at a price lower than its book value.

Capital stock is ordinarily classified as common and preferred. Common stock represents the original and residual rights of ownership. Preferred stock also represents ownership but has certain rights and privileges not enjoyed by the common stock. Thus, preferred stock is ordinarily entitled to a certain fixed amount of dividends before any distribution is made to the common stock, and it may also be entitled to a prior amount in the distribution of assets when the company is liquidated. Preferred stock generally has no voting power but may acquire it if its dividends are not paid. In addition, preferred stock may be cumulative or non-cumulative. If it is cumulative, it has a prior claim for its fixed dividend for each year in which the dividend was not paid. If it is non-cumulative it has a prior claim only to the current year's profits.

16. *Par value capital stock.* Capital stock may have a par, or face, value or it may have no par value. If it is par value stock, a certain fixed number of dollars is printed on the stock certificate. Such stock may be authorized and issued at $1.00 par, $10.00 par, $100.00 par or any other amount authorized by the charter.

At one time, it was assumed that when shares of stock were issued, the total value was represented by tangible assets of exactly the same value. With the introduction of intangible assets such as organization expense, promotion expense, and good will, the par value has become only theoretically an indication of the tangible values in the business. Furthermore, the subterfuge previously described, whereby the capital stock was made full paid by issuance for property or services, opened the way toward a complete divorcement of the par value of the stock and its intrinsic value.

17. *No par value capital stock.* In order to eliminate the necessity for this subterfuge and also to remove the dollar value from the stock certificate, so that the un-wary purchaser might not believe that the par value represented full tangible value, a series of laws were passed by the various states, authorizing the issue of capital stock without par value. Such stock merely represents a share in the total net assets of the company, which share is found by dividing the net worth by the number of shares issued.

Provision is made in these laws whereby a "stated value" may be used for tax purposes, and to denote the amount of the owner's equity in the net assets. No par stock may be sold for whatever it will bring, and is always full-paid and non-assessable. While this feature permits easier financing, it is to some extent undesirable because of the fact that shares may be offered at different prices. This may result in an anomalous method of recording the capital stock in the books, and a doubtful feeling on the part of the purchaser.

No par stock has probably not entirely eliminated the features of par value stock that led to its inauguration. The elimination of the dollar mark from the stock certificate does not prevent the unscrupulous salesman from using persuasive methods and exaggerated statements concerning the value of the certificates which he has for sale. Nor does the use of no par stock entirely prevent the inflation of property book values. In fact, insofar as the relationship between the promoters and the creditors is concerned, there is much argument for par value stock. If the creditors lose money and can prove that, at the inception of the enterprise, the company did not receive full value up to the par value of the stock issued, they have a right to recover by action at law. Their right to recover in the case of no par stock is much more difficult to prove.

18. *Long-term borrowing.* A portion of the capital of a corporation may be obtained by long-term borrowing. When bonds are issued, they appear in the balance sheet directly under the

capital stock. While they are a direct liability of the corporation, they are listed separately from the short-term debt because they are a part of the permanent capitalization. A study of the bonds is important for two reasons: first, because the type of bond that has been issued is important to the purchaser; and second, because the relationship of the amount of capital borrowed to the total capitalization may have marked effect upon the financial status of the enterprise. The reason for the importance of the latter is described in a later chapter.

Bonds may be classified with regard to their security, or to the purposes for which they are issued. Thus, bonds may be secured or unsecured. The chief forms of secured bonds are the mortgage bonds and the collateral trust bonds. The mortgage bond is secured by a mortgage on real property, which mortgage may be a first mortgage, or it may be subject to a prior lien or liens. First mortgage bonds are most favored by investors, and bring the best prices when sold by the corporation. Some mortgage bonds are secured only in part by a first mortgage, the balance of the security being a second or even a third mortgage. These are known as first and refunding mortgage bonds and are issued for the purpose of ultimately refunding other prior securities. They gradually become first mortgage bonds as the previous issues are paid.

19. *Collateral trust bonds.* Some bonds are secured by deposits of other securities with a trustee who holds a deed of trust. These are known as collateral trust bonds. Usually, the securities pledged under a collateral trust agreement are those of subsidiary companies, the income from which is used in part or in whole to pay the interest upon the collateral trust bonds. This type of bond is quite generally used by railroads and public utilities, but is rarely used by industrial companies.

20. *Unsecured bonds.* Unsecured bonds are known as debentures. Their only security is the general credit of the corporation, and, except that they are long-term obligations, they have the same status as other unsecured creditors such as accounts and notes payable. Because investors in the past have been wary of debenture bonds. their interest rates have generally been higher than those of mortgage bonds. The investor has not been completely wise in his attitude because the debenture bonds of a strong corporation should not be subject to such discrimination. The safety of bonds is dependent more upon the ability of the corporation to earn sufficient profits, and, in turn, to pay the interest and finally the principal, than upon the value of the lien attaching to the bonds. In many cases, if insolvency comes, the investor will be able to exercise his legal rights under a lien only with doubt and delay.

The Interpretation of the Balance Sheet Pt 2.

1. *The analysis of the fixed assets.* The analysis of the fixed assets is concerned largely with their size. When the fixed assets are small in proportion to the total investment in the business, there is usually no particular problem, especially if the business is producing a fair profit. Fixed assets of small amount should be checked to determine whether their size is because of the type of business or the result of a decision of the management to rent plant facilities rather than to invest capital in their purchase. If the company is paying rent, an estimate should be made as to the annual cost, because the rental paid may be greater than the cost of obtaining the additional capital necessary to purchase a plant.

Under any circumstances, the financial problems arising from a small investment in fixed assets are by no means as great as those arising from overinvestment. Excessive fixed assets cause financial troubles and a condition that is difficult to overcome. Inventories which have piled up, and overdue accounts receivable, may, within a comparatively short space of time, be reduced by selling at a discount in the case of the former; or by offering reductions in the amount due in the case of the latter. When, however, excessive plant has resulted in a "frozen" capital situation, years may be required to remedy it.

2. *Results of excessive investment in fixed assets.* Excessive investment in fixed assets causes continuous pressure to increase sales so that a satisfactory return may be made on the investment. The expansion of plant, paid for out of earnings, drains working capital, and eventually leads to a serious current situation; even insolvency may result. The depreciation alone, on an excessively large plant, so greatly reduces profits that companies seek drastic means to overcome it. Of late, this has resulted in large charge-offs of fixed assets for the sole purpose of reducing the depreciation charge. While profits may be increased in this manner, the increase is not a true profit, and the normal annual loss due to depreciation continues. In the long run, the cure may be worse than the disease.

How serious the excessive investment in fixed assets becomes depends in part upon the methods used in financing the company. If the capital has been obtained entirely by the sale of common stock, the troubles may be at a minimum, with merely some loss of dividends by the stockholders. When, however, bonds and mortgages have been used in the financial plan, trouble is almost certain to ensue. Because of the costs of maintaining an excessively large plant, profits may be affected to the extent that there may be difficulty in meeting periodic interest payments. Out of this may arise some doubt as to the ability of the company to pay the principal of its obligations at maturity.

Worst of all, however, is the situation which exists when the plant financing has been made at the expense of the working capital. No enterprise can long endure if it lacks sufficient working capital to finance its normal production. It is patent, therefore, that the analyst consider, along with the size of the fixed assets, the condition of the working capital so that he can determine whether or not a substantial part of it has become frozen in fixed assets.

3. *Definition of working capital.* Working capital is the total of the current assets less the current liabilities. Some writers make a distinction between gross and net working capital, defining the former as the total of the current assets, and the latter as the difference between the current assets and the current liabilities. The former definition is used in this text.

The amount of working capital which is necessary varies with the individual enterprise. If the business has a relatively high percentage of cash sales, the need for working capital is less than in the case of one which must sell to all its customers on a time basis. The length of time of the manufacturing process and the normal credit period are also factors. Furthermore, the type of raw material is not without its effect, because the amount of working capital needed to finance inventories which must be purchased in large amounts, at infrequent periods, is greater than when inventories may be purchased as needed.

Adequate working capital is that amount which enables the business to operate efficiently from day to days which will carry the business through its seasonal demands, and which is sufficient to supply enough funds to take care of normal increases in the demand for in product. It is not usually necessary to provide in advance for additional working capital which may be needed for increased demand due to cyclical changes although many corporations in planning their finances obtain surplus capital at the outset. The danger of having too much working capital lying around is that waste is encouraged, and there is always the possibility that the temptation to speculate may become too great for the management.

4. *How temporary working capital is obtained.* Working capital which is needed for a temporary situation may be obtained by short-term borrowing. Such temporary working capital should not be obtained by the sale of bonds because the fixed charges thereby incurred may seriously handicap the corporation after the immediate necessity has passed. The result of obtaining temporary working capital by the sale of preferred stock is less serious, but here also, the corporation may find itself in an embarrassing relationship with its common stockholders if it is necessary to reduce their dividends in order to pay dividends on the preferred stock.

The sufficiency of the working capital must be tested by a quantitative study of the current assets and current liabilities. In addition, the total capital of the corporation must be studied to determine the proportion invested in fixed assets as compared with the net current assets. Working capital cannot be satisfactorily studied except in its relation to the financial status of the enterprise as a whole.

5. *Causes of inadequate working capital.* If the analyst believes that the amount of working capital is inadequate, he attempts to diagnose the cause by a study of the income accounts and balance sheets for a period of years. Decreasing working capital comes about through a number of causes, of which operating loss is probably the most common. A corporation which has been losing money over a period of years quite naturally suffers a decrease in its assets, and the particular assets which decrease most rapidly are the current assets. Frequently, cash leads the downward march.

Losses of an extraordinary nature, which are frequently non-recurrent, may also have a drastic effect upon the working capital. A number of years ago, the losses sustained by many corporations in the Ohio Valley, due to the severe floods, were sufficient to place some of them at least temporarily in a precarious financial condition. Again, losses due to strikes may have a similar effect. Indeed, most extraordinary losses, if they are large, seriously affect the working capital position because it is usually not possible to fully insure against such losses.

The freezing of current funds in fixed assets, that is by financing from current funds rather than by the sale of additional capital stock, and a continuous policy of reducing preferred stock and bonds, also cause severe drains on the working capital. Where such policies are in effect, the analyst must consider how long the corporation can withstand the strain, and whether financial troubles are in the offing.

Mere profits do not make the payment of dividends possible. Profits to be available for dividends must remain in assets which can be liquidated and produce cash without affecting the continuance of satisfactory production. If the "liquid" assets are not sufficient to pay the dividend, current borrowing may furnish the necessary funds if the working capital position is strong, Such borrowing, however, should be done only when there is speedy turnover of inventories and of accounts receivable in order that prompt settlement of the debt may be possible. The analyst studies the dividend policy of the corporation to determine whether dividends are paid with or without due consideration to the working capital position.

6. *The cash position.* Having examined the working capital in total, the analyst turns his attention to the individual accounts. No general rule can be laid down as to the amount of cash which should be on hand. Many factors must be considered: the type of the industry, the length of the manufacturing process, the length of the credit period, and the nature and amount of the current liabilities. In addition, the long-term debt must be examined to determine whether a cash reserve is necessary to furnish funds to redeem obligations which mature in the near future.

The sufficiency of cash is a matter of judgment on the part of the analyst after he has considered the speed of the turnover of the business. The time involved in converting inventories into finished goods, together with the velocity with which accounts receivable are turned into cash, determines the turnover. If the business is seasonal in nature, consideration must be given to the date of the statements, whether they are issued at the peak of production or during the off season.

7. *Testing the receivables.* The accounts receivable must be tested as completely as possible, consistent with the data on hand. If the analyst has access to information concerning the various accounts, he can determine their value very closely. On the other hand, if he has only the statements before him, he is able only to estimate their value from the relationship between the sales and the receivables. A method frequently used is to reduce the sales to an average daily basis. The average daily sales is then applied to the outstanding accounts receivable.

Thus, for example, if a corporation had sales of $1,260,000 in a given year, the average daily sales is found by dividing by 360 days. The average daily sales of $3,500 thus obtained is applied to the accounts receivable which, at the end of the year, showed a balance of $52,500. Dividing $52,500 by $3,500 gives 15 which indicates the average number of days during which the accounts have been outstanding. If the normal credit period of the company is approximately two weeks, the turnover of accounts receivable would be deemed to be satisfactory. If, however, it so happened that the average duration of the accounts showed 60 days, the turnover would be considered extremely slow.

This test is complicated at times because there are large amounts of notes receivable. If these notes have been received from customers in the usual course of the operations of the business, they must be considered together with the accounts receivable. Sometimes, the notes receivable account contains notes received because of transactions other than those resulting from sales of the product. If this is the case, the test is not as specific, but it nevertheless gives a rough indication of the speed at which the customers' accounts are being collected.

8. *Testing the reserve for bad debts.* The accounts receivable may be further tested by means of a study of the reserve for bad debts. In order that losses from uncollectible accounts may be included in the profit and loss for the year to which they belong, it is usual to deduct from the profits each year an estimated amount for bad debts. The reserve for bad debts thus provided remains in the balance sheet, and is reduced by the amount of uncollectible items as they occur. The reserve for bad debts should be tested as to its use and as to its adequacy in amount. In the normal business, a reservation annually amounting to two to five per cent of the outstanding accounts receivable is usually considered sufficient.

An investigation of the amount of bad debts actually occurring, however, may cause the analyst to revise the valuation of the accounts receivable. This amount may be determined if the income account shows the annual credit to the reserve. If, however, the annual charge for bad debts is hidden in the general and administrative expenses, the analyst has only the balance of the reserve as shown in the balance sheet to work with, and this does not give sufficient data for an adequate check.

To test the annual allowance for bad debts, a simple application of the amount in the income account to the balance of the receivables is all that is necessary. This shows the percentage of the accounts receivable which has been set aside from profits to take care of debts that may become uncollectible. To find the amount of the reserve for bad debts which has actually been used, an additional calculation is necessary.

Suppose that the balance of the reserve for bad debts is shown in the 1950 balance sheet as $100,000, and that the 1951 income account shows that $10,000 was reserved from the 1951 profits. The balance sheet for the year 1951 should thus show a reserve for bad debts with a balance of $110,000, provided no use was made of the reserve during that year. If, however, the balance of the reserve for bad debts in the 1951 balance sheet was only $95,000, then $15,000 of the reserve was used in eliminating uncollectible accounts from the books during the year 1951. If the use of the reserve over a period of years appears to be excessive, and an increase in the annual charge against profits is indicated, the analyst makes allowance for this in his estimate of the company's financial condition.

9. *Excessive accounts and notes receivable.* Excessive accounts receivable may be a temporary condition brought about by the state of business in the industry. In such a case, the going may be difficult for a time, but the situation may eventually correct itself. An abnormally poor corn crop, for instance, may place such a financial burden upon farmers that they are able to pay their obligations on time only with great difficulty. Enterprises which have extended credit to these farmers are forced to make allowances as to the time of payment, but, eventually, the actual losses may be small.

When, however, accounts receivable become excessive because sales are decreasing and poorer risks are being taken in order to stem the downward trend, a more serious situation occurs. In the first instance, the risks were originally good, but, because of extraordinary conditions, the accounts became slow-moving. In the latter case, the risks were originally poor and are likely, therefore, to result in an abnormal percentage of losses. The notes receivable should not normally be large unless the business is one in which notes, or trade acceptances, are the rule rather than the exception. Where this is true, the accounts receivable are generally smaller in proportion. If both accounts and notes receivable show substantial balances, the analyst may be suspicious that the notes represent evidences of indebtedness which may have been forced from past due accounts, or worse, that they represent debts of officers or employees of the company.

10. *Excessive inventories.* The inventory is likely to be the largest of the current assets, and the one which moves the slowest toward cash. The analyst looks for indications of excessive

inventories which may cause the enterprise to operate under a serious financial handicap, or for evidence of inventory shortage which may result in reduced profits because customers are not supplied promptly. The latter is the less frequent condition.

Excessive inventories are not only serious because they are likely to result in losses, but also because of the amount of capital tied up in them. Inventories carried for a long time deteriorate in value, some types more than others, but the more serious problem which arises from over-stocking is the financial one. Large purchases must be financed, and, if the working capital is not liquid enough, or not sufficient, the financing must come from borrowing, or by extension of credit by the vendors. Either of these affects the working capital position adversely, since current liabilities are increased.

The analyst should study the type of business in order to estimate the amount of inventory which a corporation must carry. He should consider the length of time necessary for the manufacture of the product, and the amount of time necessary to make sales and to collect the accounts receivable. A business which needs only a small amount of raw materials per unit of product, the manufacturing process of which takes but a few hours, and which has constant demand from its customers, has modest inventory requirements. No large amount of capital is necessary and no excessive inventories should be involved.

On the other hand, a business which requires several months to fabricate its product, which uses large amounts of raw material and labor, and which sells on credit terms of ninety days or more, has all the elements which demand a large working capital, including a high proportion of inventories. The financial plan of such a business must be arranged so as to meet the situation.

The question of price stability in the raw material market must also be considered. When the raw materials vary little in price, there should be little need for the purchase of inventories in advance of their use, in order to take advantage of low prices. If, however, inventories fluctuate regularly in price, the analyst must satisfy himself that the corporation is not purchasing excessively. A policy of purchasing when prices are low is exemplary provided great care is used. If, however, there is lack of forethought in the purchasing policy, a swift and severe fall in prices, coupled with a diminishing demand, may be devastating to the enterprise, particularly if that policy calls for excessive short-term borrowing.

11. *The Liabilities.* The liabilities present two problems: first, their classification for purposes of analysis; and second, the possibility that all of them may not appear in the balance sheet. The analyst separates the liabilities into three classes. The first class includes those which are part of the invested capital of the enterprise, namely, all bonds, mortgages, and capital obligations which are due more than a year from the date of the balance sheet. In the second class are the current liabilities. These include the accounts and notes payable, loans payable, taxes accrued,

and dividends which have been declared but not paid. The deferred items and the various reserves make up the third class.

The liabilities must be carefully scanned for accounts which are, in effect, current liabilities, but which have been included among the deferred items. A reserve for taxes, for instance, is a current liability, but is likely to be listed with the other reserves. To omit it from the current liabilities would give an erroneous impression of the working capital.

12. *Contingent liabilities.* Whether the liabilities, as listed in the balance sheet, include all the liabilities is a question which the analyst may not be able to answer unless he has access to the corporate records. He must, however, read the company's statements and the certificate of the accountants carefully, in order to determine whether contingent liabilities exist. From a strict accounting standpoint, all contingent liabilities should be included in the balance sheet, but, as a practical matter, they are frequently excluded, although a foot note may indicate their existence.

The custom of omitting the contingent liability upon discounted notes receivable may result, on occasion, in "window-dressing" the working capital. When a corporation discounts the notes of its customers at its bank, it becomes contingently liable to pay the bank the face value of the notes in case they are not paid by the makers. To show this transaction in full in the books, accounting rules demand that the notes receivable be retained among the assets until their due dates, and that they be offset on the liability side of the balance sheet by an account "Notes Receivable Discounted."

There is some objection to this procedure because an amount no longer owned by the company is included in the assets, and a like amount which may not have to be paid is included in the liabilities. Furthermore, this procedure results in a relationship between current assets and the total current liabilities which may be misleading. Therefore, it is frequently advocated that, in the balance sheet, no recognition be given to the contingency other than by a footnote.

13. *Illustration of "window-dressing" the working capital.* The following illustration will explain how it is possible to "window-dress" the working capital.

Company X has far from a satisfactory working capital position. It has little cash, its accounts receivable are much too high, and its accounts payable are excessive. The management, desiring to present a more favorable statement, requests customers, whose accounts are due or past-due to give promissory notes for their balances. These notes will probably be non-interest-bearing, and discounts may even be offered in order to assure acceptance of the plan.

The company now obtains cash by discounting the notes at its bank, the cash being used in the payment of some of the accounts payable.

The working capital position is now apparently satisfactory, with current assets of $20,800 and current liabilities of only $8,000. By the simple expedient of discounting notes, the company has apparently turned a situation in which it had little over a dollar of current assets for each dollar of current liabilities into one in which there are $2.60 of current assets for each dollar of current liabilities. If all the notes are paid by their makers, when they come due, the situation will remain satisfactory. If, however, the notes should not be paid, the company will End itself with a liability to its bank of $20,000, and with only $4,800 of cash to meet it. The importance of information concerning contingent liabilities is apparent. Absence of such information may give a false impression of the liquidity of the business.

14. *Capitalization of the enterprise.* The asset side of the balance sheet contains the assets with which the business endeavors to earn a profit. The liability side contains the sources from which the necessary capital has been obtained. Capital comes from the owners of the business who are represented by the capital stock accounts, and from the creditors who are represented by the accounts and notes payable, bonds, and other obligations.

The business should be operated in such a manner as to make sufficient profit to pay not only the interest on its obligations, but also the principal of these obligations, and, in addition, return to the owners a fair profit upon their investment. It follows, then, that the proportion of capital invested by the owners in relation to the total capital in use is of some importance. The corporation undertakes to pay only a limited amount of interest upon its borrowed capital, but expects no limit to be set upon the profits which accrue to the stockholders. The owners, that is the stockholders, of the enterprise proceed upon the assumption that their share of the profits should be larger than the interest on borrowed funds because of the greater risk which they assume.

15. *Trading on the equity.* The desire for greater profits on the part of the owners frequently leads to a speculative financial plan which transfers a greater part of the risk to the creditors. This plan increases the proportion of borrowed capital to the total capital.

Under normal conditions, the investment of the stockholders provides a cushion for the safety of the creditors, because the greater the amount of the stockholders' interest, the greater care will they take to operate the corporation efficiently, and safeguard that interest. When the proportion of borrowed capital becomes excessive, the stockholders have relatively less at stake, and the risk begins to be transferred to the creditors. When a large amount of capital is obtained by borrowing at an interest rate which is considerably lower than the rate of return upon the total capital through the operation of the business, the stockholders are said to be "trading on the equity."

The share of the profits paid to the bondholders has a specified limit, but the stockholders have a claim upon the entire balance of the profits after that share has been paid. The term profits is here used in the sense of the total return from the operations of the business, before the payment of the fixed charges. The stockholders, therefore, may speculate or gamble for higher profits by limiting the amount of their own investment, and, at the same time, increasing the amount of borrowed capital.

The great danger in this speculation arises from the fact that the high fixed charges, resulting from the over-issuance of bonds, may not be earned if business declines. This may result in insolvency or a receivership. Furthermore, the reaction of the stock market to the securities of the company may have an effect upon its ability to obtain additional capital in the future. Because of this latter fact, the market quotations of a company's securities should be more the concern of the management than that usually assumed.

16. *Example of trading on the equity.* The following example illustrates the effect of trading on the equity. The balance sheets are of two companies earning a like amount, and having the same net tangible values; one capitalized entirely by means of common stock, and the other by capital stock and bonds.

Suppose that each of these companies in a certain year earned $100,000 before fixed charges and dividends. The per share earnings of Company A is calculated by dividing $100,000 by 10,000, the number of shares. Company A thus earned $10 per share. The situation in Company B is quite different. The common stock is entitled to earnings only after the prior obligation of bond interest has been paid. The interest of $24,000 on the bonds must first be deducted from the $100,000. The remaining balance of $76,000 is then available for the common stock. Company B has only 4,000 shares of stock, so that each share earned $19 as compared with $10 in the case of Company A.

If the directors of the two companies are fairly liberal in their dividend policies, and declare dividends up to about 60% of the earnings, the stockholders of Company A may expect to receive a dividend of $6 as compared with a probable dividend of about $11 for the stockholders of Company B. If profits should rise, the advantage accruing to the stockholders of Company B is greater percentagewise than that accruing to the stockholders of Company A. Thus, if the profits should reach $200,000, the earnings per share of Company A would increase to $20, but the earnings per share of Company B would rise to $44.

17. *The danger of trading on the equity.* As long as profits increase or remain high, trading on the equity rewards the common stockholder handsomely, but there are other implications. When profits decrease, the proportionate loss to the stockholders of a corporation which is trading on the equity is greater than to the stockholders of a corporation which has not used borrowed capital. Using the previous illustration, suppose that the profits of the two companies dropped to $40,000. The per share earnings of the stock of Company A would be $4, and the

per share earnings of Company B would be exactly the same. This would represent a decrease of 60% in the per share earnings of Company A, and a 79% decrease in the case of Company B.

Excessive trading on the equity is speculative and dangerous for the stockholders; furthermore, it does not give adequate protection to the bondholders. The inevitable result is that neither the bonds nor the stock bring the prices in the stock market which the company might deserve if it were capitalized on a more conservative basis. Because of the fact that the market quotations of common stocks frequently follow the current earnings per share, it has been possible for corporations to influence these prices by simple adjustments in capitalization.

It is possible, for instance, to increase the per share earnings of the common stock by the introduction of bonds in the capital structure. The increase of the per share earnings will be reflected in the market price of the stock. Too many changes in the capital structure of a corporation create the suspicion that there may have been speculation by the corporation, or its officers, in its capital stock.

18. *Preferred stock also results in trading on the equity.* What has been stated concerning the use of bonds in the capital structure applies in part to the use of preferred stock. Since the preferred stock dividend is fixed, it has the same effect upon common stock earnings as bond interest. There is this difference, however: the non-payment of bond interest forces a declaration of insolvency, or a receivership, but the passing of a preferred dividend may do no more than force a change of management through the resulting shift of voting power from the common to the preferred stock. Most preferred stock obtains voting power if a certain number of dividends are not paid.

In some of the financing of public utilities in the 1920's, trading on the equity was carried to its most excessive state; preferred stocks and bonds of many classes were piled on top of the common stock, which frequently was not only of small amount but also had the sole voting power. In this manner, public utility managements were able to obtain maximum profits with minimum investments. In the depression years which followed, however, many of these common stock equities were completely wiped out.

19. *Changes in capitalization.* In studying the capitalization of the corporation, the analyst takes careful note of the changes of the past, and studies the probable effect of possible changes in the future. If a study is made of the earnings per share of the common stock for a period of years, it must include whatever changes have been made in the number of shares. Generally a recalculation of the earnings per share is necessary.

Thus, for example, if a corporation, with 10,000 shares outstanding, averaged $100,000 earnings over a period of years, the average earnings per share would be $10; but if the number of shares outstanding was 20,000, the average per share would be only $5. In order to study the per share earnings for a period of years, adjustment must be made for changes in capitalization in order that each year may be upon a comparable basis. The arithmetical average of the reported earnings per share does not give the true picture because the number of shares in two of the years was 10,000, while, in three of the years, it was 12,000. By adjusting the whole five-year period to the 12,000-share basis, the analyst is able to determine the per share earning power of the company under its present capitalization.

An estimate of future changes in capitalization is also of great importance. This is particularly true where the analyst has means of anticipating what changes will take place. Assume that a corporation has 5,000 shares of 5% preferred stock and 10,000 shares of common stock outstanding, and that the preferred is convertible into 1% shares of common stock. Assume further that the company has been earning an average of $100,000 per annum before fixed charges and dividends.

Before the conversion privilege is exercised, the earnings available for the common stock are $100,000, less the preferred dividend of $25,000, or $75,000. The per share earnings of the common stock thus amount to $7.50. If, however, the preferred stockholders exercise the conversion privilege, the number of common shares will increase to 17,500. The earnings of $100,000 available for the common stock will now be only $5.71 per share, and the price of the stock in the market may be expected to reflect this change. It is true that these calculations are of primary importance to the investor, but, as has been previously stated, they are not without significance to the management which has to consider the manner in which future capital will be provided.

Advisory 4

Consolidated Statements

1. *Consolidations.* Corporations frequently purchase the stocks and bonds of other corporations. The object of such purchases may be to invest surplus working capital temporarily, or to invest surplus over-all capital in long-term securities. Again, it may be to secure control of other companies for the purpose of obtaining a continuous source of raw materials or supplies, or to effect other economies in operations. When control of another corporation is obtained, the two corporations are to all intents and purposes a single enterprise although each keeps its own corporate identity.

2. *Parent and subsidiary companies.* The "Stocks and Bonds" or "Investments" account of a corporation listed among the assets, may thus include two types of securities, those representing a controlling interest in other corporations, and those which are the result of casual purchases of stocks and bonds. Since the controlled company, or subsidiary company, as it is commonly known, is an essential part of the parent company, or purchasing company, no analysis is complete unless the accounts of both companies are scrutinized. This is not as difficult as it would seem because most parent companies issue what are known as consolidated statements. A consolidated statement is one which include, the accounts of the parent company and the subsidiary company or companies, with the exception of certain accounts which are strictly inter-company in character.

3. **_The purpose of the consolidated statement._** The purpose of the consolidated statement is to show the complete financial facts of two or more related companies as if they were one company. Since the companies are related, there are usually inter-company transactions. Furthermore, since the companies keep their separate corporate identities, their financial records are kept separately. Thus, an inter-company transaction is entered upon the books of both companies. Only at the time of the preparation of the financial statements are the data consolidated or brought together. At such a time, adjustments are necessary in the case of the inter-company accounts in order to prevent duplication.

Thus, for example, if Company A, which owns 100% of the capital stock of Company B, buys inventory from Company B on account, Company A increases its inventory by the amount of the purchase and shows an account payable to Company B. Company B, on the other hand, records a sale to Company A, and sets up an account receivable with it. From the standpoint of the individual corporations, these entries are necessary, but, if it is desired to combine the accounts of the two companies in financial statements as if there were only one company, it is necessary to eliminate the amount of the sale, the purchase, and the resulting accounts receivable and payable. As a unit, no goods have been sold and nothing is either due or payable.

4. **_Combined statements._** It is a relatively simple matter to construct a combined income account, or a combined balance sheet, of a parent and its subsidiary company or companies. Such a statement merely contains all the financial figures of the companies in one statement. Such a statement, however, would be difficult to read and interpret because of the numerous inter-company accounts. The consolidated statements seek to eliminate all such duplications, and to show the financial situation of the controlling interest, that is, from the standpoint of the stockholders of the parent company.

The construction of consolidated statements is based on certain definite principles which, while they are by no means simple, nevertheless result in a satisfactory type of statement. These basic principles are explained in the illustrations which follow. No attempt has been made to cover all the variations of corporate stock ownership, but sufficient illustrations are given to demonstrate how consolidated statements are constructed. Since a large proportion of the published statements of corporations whose shares are listed on the stock exchanges are consolidated statements, it is important that the analyst understands how they are constructed.

5. **_Full control purchased at the book value of the net assets._** The balance sheets of three companies follow. The Philadelphia Company has purchased the entire capital stock of both the Atlanta Company and the Boston Corporation. Each of the companies has kept its corporate identity, but the directors of the Atlanta Company and the Boston Corporation are representatives of the Philadelphia Company. The capital stock of the subsidiary companies has

been purchased at a price equal to the book value of the net assets. The book value of the capital stock of a corporation is the total of the capital stock plus the surplus.

The book value of the capital stock of the Atlanta Company was, therefore, $300,000, the total of its capital stock and surplus; likewise, the book value of the capital stock of the Boston Corporation was $350,000. The purchase price of these stocks ($300,000 plus $350,000) appears as an asset in the balance sheet of the Philadelphia Company.

While these three companies keep their separate corporate identities, keep their own books and records, and issue their own financial statements, they are in effect one organization and must, therefore, be analyzed as one unit.

Such a statement, while it has some advantages over three separate statements, contains certain duplications. The stocks and bonds account among the assets represents the purchase of the capital stock and surplus accounts of the Atlanta Company and the Boston Corporation. No good purpose is served by this duplication, and, furthermore, the stockholders and management of the Philadelphia Company are interested in the assets and the liabilities of these companies, and not in their capital accounts. Therefore, the statement can be simplified by eliminating the duplications. Despite these eliminations, the total assets and total liabilities of the three companies are included in the statement.

This statement contains the information concerning the project as a whole. The assets of the three companies, their liabilities, and the equity of the stockholders of the parent company are all included. It should be understood, of course, that the assets and liabilities would be listed in detail; they are shown here in totals only for purposes of simplification.

6. *Full control purchased at a price greater than the book value of the net assets.* The foregoing illustration was based upon the fact that the parent company purchased the full capital stocks of the subsidiary companies at exactly their book value. This rarely happens in practice. Suppose that the Philadelphia Company purchased the full capital stock of the Atlanta Company at a price of $500,000.

The book value of the capital stock of the Atlanta Company is $300,000. The Philadelphia Company has paid $500,000 for this book value, or $200,000 in excess of the book value. If the Philadelphia Company has been willing to pay such a price, it must assume that the net assets are worth more than their book value. The Atlanta Company has good will, which is not expressed in its accounts, and the holders of the capital stock are entitled to payment therefor. This good will becomes an asset of the parent company, and thus appears in its balance sheet.

7. *Full control purchased at a price less than the book value of the net assets.* A corporation is quite as likely to purchase an interest in a subsidiary company for an amount less

than book value. Suppose that the Philadelphia Company purchased the entire capital stock of the Boston Corporation for $250,000.

The book value of the capital stock of the Boston Corporation is $350,000. The Philadelphia Company was able to buy this book value for $250,000. Thus. it obtains an additional $100,000 in value which must be laced in its accounts and in its balance sheet. This additional value is surplus, but it must not be confused with earned surplus since it is not available for dividends. The account is properly named capital surplus, and explains the additional amount which has been added to the assets.

8. *The consolidated balance sheet when less than full control is acquired.* Thus far, it has been assumed that the parent company has purchased the entire capital stocks of the subsidiary companies. This does not usually happen. A corporation may obtain 51% of the capital stock of a subsidiary company, and have undoubted control.

On the other hand, it is possible to have effective control when less than 50% of the capital stock is purchased. This happens when the capital stock of the subsidiary company is held by a large number of persons. Because of the wide distribution, it is unlikely that a competing group might obtain control of a significant number of shares. Therefore, 40% or even 35% of the capital stock might be an effective majority. When the amount of the capital stock purchased is less than 50%, it is a matter for the judgment of the accountants as to whether the balance sheets be consolidated, or whether to the capital stock of the subsidiary company be ether included in the stocks and bonds account of the parent company.

Let us now suppose that the Philadelphia Company was able to purchase 90% of the capital stock of the Boston Corporation for $300,000.

Here is another instance of capital surplus resulting from the purchase of capital stock at less than its book value, but, in this instance, there is an additional factor. The parent company has not purchased all the capital stock of the subsidiary. Some of it is still in the hands of persons who have no relationship to the parent company. From the standpoint of the parent company, these persons represent a minority interest, and there is no reason for the inclusion of that interest in a consolidated statement except for the fact that all the holders of capital stock have equities in the net assets of the companies.

Whether the stockholder is a member of a majority group or a minority group is of no consequence, his rights are the same. And because the full value of all the assets and all the liabilities of the subsidiary company must be shown in the consolidated balance sheet, the parent company cannot claim that it owns 90% of any particular asset, or that it is liable for only 90% of any particular liability; just as the minority stockholders cannot claim ownership of 10% of the cash, or a liability for only 10% of the accounts payable, It is thus necessary to include in the consolidated statement not only all the assets and all the liabilities but also all the claims against the net assets.

Sometimes the details of the minority interest are not shown, but the total is merely carried in the consolidated balance sheet under the caption "Minority Interests in Subsidiary Companies."

9. *Profits and losses in consolidated balance sheets.* After the purchase of a controlling interest in a subsidiary company, both the parent company and the subsidiary company continue to operate, and each keeps its own financial records. At the end of the fiscal year, each company reports its own profits or losses, and constructs its own statements. When the ensuing consolidated balance sheet is constructed, it is necessary to adjust the surplus account of the parent company in order to absorb the profit or loss of the subsidiary company.

Let us assume that the purchase on 90% of the stock of the Boston Corporation took place on or about January 2, 1951. Let us assume further that the Philadelphia Company made a profit of $15,000 in the year 1951, while the Boston Corporation made a profit of $5,000.

Since a profit was made and the surplus has increased, there would necessarily be an increase in the net assets; that is, either the assets would have increased or the liabilities would have decreased, or there would have been a combination of the two. For simplicity, it is assumed that all the increase was in the assets.

The $15,000 earnings of the Philadelphia Company are now included, of course, in the surplus account of that company. But the Philadelphia Company has also an interest in the earnings of the Boston Corporation by virtue of its ownership of 90% of the capital stock. Since the net assets of the Boston Corporation have increased by $5,000, or the amount of its earnings, its surplus account will show a like increase.

This addition of $5,000 must be divided into the portion to which the majority interest is entitled, and that to which the minority interest has a claim. The amount of the former is $4,500, while that of the latter is $500. The earned surplus of the parent company has increased, therefore, from $100,000 to $119,500, the increase consisting of its own earnings plus ninety per cent of the earnings of its subsidiary. Likewise, the surplus of the minority interest has increased from $5,000 to $5,500 because of its proportion of the earnings.

When a corporation owns a considerable amount of stock in another company but does not have a controlling interest, it usually does not consolidate its statements, but carries the investment in its assets under an appropriate caption. Sometimes, the value at which the investment is carried is adjusted to show the profits or losses reported. Thus, the du Pont Company, which owns a large number of shares of the General Motors Corporation, adjusts its investment in that company each year in accordance with the profits reported by the General Motors Corporation.

10. **_Inter-company transactions._** When companies are related one to the other, there is likely to be a substantial number of transactions between them. When one company buys materials from the other, or sells materials to the other, such purchases or sales are entered on the books of both companies exactly the same as if no relationship existed between them. Such transactions result in accounts receivable on the books of one company, and accounts payable on the books of the other company. When the balance sheets are consolidated, these inter-company accounts are eliminated, because the inclusion of an asset with an offsetting liability, both representing transactions of the consolidated interests, would serve no useful purpose.

This, however, does not complete the adjustments. When one of the corporations sold materials to the other, it took a profit on the transaction. It is entitled to this profit as an individual company. If the purchasing company has sold these materials to its customers, it likewise is entitled to its profit. If, however, the purchasing company has not sold the materials and still carries them in its inventory, then, from the standpoint of the consolidation, no profit has yet been realized. Unless this inter-company profit is eliminated from the combined income accounts, profits will be inflated on the one hand, and inventory values inflated on the other.

On December 15, 1951, the subsidiary company sold merchandise to the parent company for $20,000. These goods cost the subsidiary company $12,000, and resulted in a profit to if of $8,000.

On December 31, the goods thus purchased were still in the possession of Company A. When the accounts of the two companies are consolidated, the following items must be considered:

a) The purchases of the parent company (A), as of December 31, contain an amount of $20,000, the result of the inter-company transaction.
b) The sales of the subsidiary company (B) contain $20,000 for goods sold to the parent company (A), but which are still in that company's possession.
c) The inventory of the parent company (A), as of December 31. contains a profit of $8,000 charged by the subsidiary company (B). Since, from the standpoint of the consolidated interests, the goods are still on hand, this profit has not been realized.
d) The subsidiary company's (B) profit contains 8,000 which has not been realized by the consolidation.
e) The balance sheets of the two companies contain offsetting accounts receivable and payable amounting to $20,000.

In order to prevent duplication of the $20,000 sale and the $20,000 purchase, these amounts are eliminated when the income accounts are consolidated.

In a like manner, the $8,000 profit is eliminated from the inventory of the parent company (A), and the profit of the subsidiary company (B).

Furthermore, the inter-company accounts receivable and payable are eliminated from the consolidated balance sheet.

11. *Disadvantages of the consolidated statement.* Under certain conditions, the consolidated balance sheet hides the real financial condition of the enterprise. It is possible that a weak financial condition of a subsidiary company, or of the parent company, may be completely offset by an excellent financial condition of the other companies. This situation would be revealed by a study of the statements of the individual companies, but it would not be apparent when the statements were consolidated.

This balance sheet appears to be quite satisfactory. There are over $2.00 of current assets for each dollar of current liabilities, and there is earned surplus. Provided the current assets do not contain excessive inventories the creditors would seem to be in a satisfactory position.

In this connection, it should be noted that the preferred stock of the subsidiary company is shown in the consolidated balance sheet because the holders of the preferred stock have a claim against the profits and also the assets of the subsidiary company, prior to the claim of the common stockholders. Inasmuch as the parent company has established its control of the subsidiary by ownership of the common stock, its claim is secondary to that of the preferred stockholders of the subsidiary company. The preferred stock claim must be indicated in the consolidated balance sheet. If, on the other hand, the parent company had bought not only the common stock of the subsidiary but also its preferred stock, the latter could be eliminated from the consolidated balance sheet in the same manner as the common stock.

An examination of the individual balance sheets of the X Company and its subsidiary reveals quite a different financial situation than that indicated by the consolidated balance sheet.

While the creditors of the subsidiary company are adequately covered by current assets, the creditors of the X Company are in no such good position. Even if all the current assets of the X Company were available in cash, the current liabilities could expect no more than a third of their claims. Furthermore, it is hardly likely that they can expect much relief from the subsidiary company because, even in liquidation, there would be $260,000 of prior claims. The creditors of the X Company would be very much misled if they were to depend upon the consolidated balance sheet for information concerning their status.

The consolidated balance sheet may also give a false sense of security to the common stockholder of the parent company. The common stockholder might obtain the impression that there was adequate surplus to permit dividends. If no dividends were declared, he might wonder as to the reason, although he should realize that surplus alone may not indicate the ability to pay them. The individual balance sheets of the parent and the subsidiary company would tell him the real story.

The current assets, while not as large in relation to the current liabilities as they might be, nevertheless, would seem to be adequate to pay a dividend of 5%.

Company Z, even if it has sufficient profits, cannot declare a dividend because it has few current assets. If the subsidiary company declares a dividend, the amount of cash which Company Z receives will have to go in large part to its creditors. The common stockholders of Company Z are, therefore. in no such favorable situation as they would be led to believe after reading the consolidated balance sheet.

The consolidated balance sheet, in the case of a large company, offers a difficult problem to the analyst because the statements of all the subsidiary companies are not usually available. Furthermore, the number of subsidiary companies may be so great as to make complete analysis too arduous a task. If, however, the analyst understands the methods that are used in the construction of the consolidated statements, he will at least be on guard as to the possible implications. A careful examination of the consolidated statements for a period of years will give him some indication of the changes which have taken place due to the marriages and divorces of the companies under his scrutiny.

Depreciation and Depletion

1. *Depreciation.* The fixed tangible assets of a business which has been in operation for some time present widely varying degrees of economic usefulness, and of relationship to their original values. All physical assets are subject to constant decay, and, despite all efforts of the management to keep them in repair, they approach inexorably the point at which they must be discarded and replaced. This decay is a fact and not a supposition, and a business must recognize its existence and provide for the time when replacements will be necessary.

2. *Depreciation defined.* The term depreciation, in a limited sense, is used to denote loss in the value of assets due to their use or enjoyment. Sometimes, however, assets have to be replaced before they have completely lost their value, because more efficient and productive assets have become available, or because changing public demand has rendered them useless for the, task for Which they were purchased. Thus, a machine may lose its value because it is operated continuously, because a new invention has resulted in a more efficient type of machine, or because there is no longer a demand for its product. Depreciation in the broader sense, therefore, includes obsolescence.

3. *Depreciation is an operating expense.* The loss in value caused by depreciation must be replaced before the enterprise can make a profit. This loss is just as much an operating expense as the payment of wages to the workers, or the cost of fuel, or power, with which the

machines are operated. It is because depreciation is an ever-present operating expense, and an important one, that separate consideration is given to it.

4. *The effect of depreciation on the accounts.* The recognition of depreciation in the accounts has two results; it reduces the profits, or increases the losses, and it reduces the book value of the assets. Some writers have contended that the latter is the more important because, if depreciation is not considered, the balance sheet shows assets at greater values than actually exist. This is no doubt important, but the fact that values have been lost and must be replaced is of much more importance. Depreciation is primarily an expense of operation, a deduction from income, and only secondarily a revaluation of fixed assets.

5. *The reserve for depreciation.* Depreciation can be placed in the accounts as a direct deduction from the fixed assets and, at the same time, as an addition to the operating expenses. To directly reduce the fixed asset accounts is highly undesirable because the cost value of the assets is then lost for balance sheet purposes. To meet this objection, it is usual to permit the assets to remain at their original figures, and to offset them with an account known as a reserve for depreciation. When the accounts are arranged in the balance sheet, the reserves for depreciation are either shown as deductions from the asset accounts, or they are listed on the liability side. In either case, the net book value of the assets is the difference between their balances and the balances of the reserves for depreciation.

6. *Calculation of depreciation.* Depreciation can be calculated in a number of ways, but, in general, it is arranged so that the entire cost of the assets will have been deducted from the profits by the end of their estimated lives. The analyst is not so much interested in the methods used in arriving at the amount of depreciation as he is in the fact that adequate depreciation is being provided, and that it is being provided out of income.

7. *Omission of depreciation.* The effect of omitting depreciation from the accounts is not only that the profits are overstated, or the losses understated, together with inclusion of non-existent values in the balance sheet, but also that there is critical effect upon profits in later years. If, for instance, machinery which has an estimated life of ten years is purchased at a cost of $10,000, roughly speaking, each of the ten years should bear one tenth of the loss. If the depreciation is properly handled in the accounts, and the estimated life is as expected, at the end of the tenth year, the balance of $10,000 in the machinery account will be offset by $10,000 in the reserve for depreciation account.

Suppose, at this point, that the machinery must be replaced. The asset account which is now a total loss can be credited, and the reserve for depreciation account can be debited. The books, therefore, show no loss for the current year. If on the other hand, depreciation has been neglected, and no reserve has been set aside from the profits during the ten years, the total balance of the asset in the tenth year must be deducted from income. Furthermore, the profits of each of the preceding nine years were overstated by at least $1,000.

8. *The nature of the reserve for depreciation*. The reserve for depreciation in most cases is merely a book adjustment, whereby a certain amount is deducted from the profits each year, thereby making that amount unavailable for dividends, and holding it in the business. No certain distinguishable assets, such as cash or securities, are earmarked for the reserve. It is merely represented by assets of various kinds in excess of the liabilities. Only in rare cases is the reserve funded; that is, represented by a fund of cash or other liquid assets to be used only for the replacement of assets. The funding of a reserve assures the company that funds will be on hand to replace assets, but it is uneconomical because funds lying idle in banks, or invested in securities, do not earn as high a rate of return as capital actively used in the operations of the business.

9. *Why the reserve helps to finance the replacement of assets.* If the reserve is merely a bookkeeping device, and contains no specially marked cash or other liquid assets, how does the enterprise finance the replacement of assets as they are retired? Theoretically, by virtue of the amounts withheld from profits during the life of the assets, the company should be in a favorable position to easily finance the purchase of the replacements. That is, the company's total financial position, and its current position in particular, should be in a more satisfactory condition than if the amounts deducted from income for depreciation had been paid to the stockholders in dividends or otherwise expended.

If the management of a company realizes the problem of depreciation and the replacement of assets, it also realizes that when these replacements become necessary, debt is most certain to increase. Replacements of assets, if a sufficient reserve has been provided, do not affect the profits, but they do affect the working capital or the amount of the debt. Consequently, the management anticipates this increase of debt by so conserving the working capital that it can withstand the strain. A policy of reducing all debt as the reserves for depreciation increase, and the assets become older, enables purchases of replacements to be made on credit without such purchases having too much effect upon the working capital.

10. *Calculating the amount of depreciation.* The amount of depreciation to be charged is always a problem to the management. If equipment was bought at a cost of $100,000, and the estimated life of ten years exactly spanned the useful life of such equipment, an allowance of $10,000 each year would be sufficient to provide enough reserve to permit the account to be charged off without disturbing the profits of the tenth year. Unfortunately, the problem is not so simple. In a period as long as ten years, prices may change radically, and the same equipment

which cost $100,000 ten years earlier may cost $150,000 when replacements are necessary. Obviously, in such a case, the installment of $10,000 per year would not be enough.

Again, the replacement of the equipment may take place long before the end of ten years, due to the fact that it has been operated a greater number of hours per day than was anticipated. Or again, it may not be possible to maintain the equipment as was planned, overtime use preventing prompt repair. If, for any of these reasons, the reserve proves to be inadequate, the extra loss must be absorbed by the profits of the current year.

In addition to these contingencies, the factor of obsolescence is always present. Competition demands that costs be held to the minimum, and an enterprise with out-of-date equipment is indeed a sorry object in a competitive market. Thus, the amount of depreciation to be charged is not determined by the mathematical calculation of dividing the cost by the estimated years of life. Something more must be added for these contingencies. How much more is a matter for the judgment of the management, and the question as to whether that judgment is sound is one that the analyst must answer.

The analyst checks his opinion with whatever data are available concerning the company's depreciation rates and those in use by the industry as a whole. In this, he is helped by the rates permitted for income tax deductions by the Department of Internal Revenue. These may be found in Bulletin "F," published by that Bureau. They include not only over-all rates for many types of industries, but also individual rates by types of machinery and other assets.

11. *The minimum annual depreciation.* Certainly, the minimum yearly depreciation for any company should be the amount that will cover the estimated expenditures upon the plant. These expenditures include the amount of the plant which must be written off, together with a reasonable amount of replacements. There is a distinction between these two amounts. The book value of the asset retired usually does not agree in amount with the cost of the replacement. The new unit may not be of the same type as the one replaced and its cost may be greater, or prices may have risen since the old unit was purchased.

For depreciation purposes, the reserve should be sufficient to cover all expenditures which are necessary to keep the plant at its productive capacity. The problem of additions and betterments to the plant is different, and is discussed in a later paragraph. When no new additions have been made to the plant, the amount which is written off against the reserve each year is not difficult to ascertain. The plant account, the annual depreciation charge as shown in the income account, and the reserve for depreciation account in the balance sheet, give the necessary information.

Thus, if the balance sheet of the reserve for depreciation account in the 1948 balance sheet was $21,400, and the company set aside $1,800 from the 1949 profits, the balance of the reserve account as of December 31, 1949 should be $23,200. But the 1949 balance sheet reveals the fact that the balance of the reserve is only $21,900. Therefore, assets amounting to $1,300 have been deducted from the reserve. In like manner, the amount of the reserve used in 1950 and 1951 is calculated, and the total of these amounts shows that the company in three years used $5,500 of its reserve for the retirement of assets. In view of the fact that the annual depreciation set aside for three years totaled only $5,700, it is apparent that the company's depreciation policy is barely adequate, and probably will become very inadequate in the future when the assets become older.

12. *Checking the replacements of assets.* A further check may be made to determine the extent to which the company is making replacements of assets that it has retired.

Thus the company, in the three years, 1949-1951 inclusive, charged off a total of $5,500 of its assets, and replaced them with assets costing $4000. The $5,500 which was charged against the reserve for depreciation is not a deduction from the profits of the three years.

The purchase of $4,000 of assets, however, must be financed, and, theoretically at least, the company should be in a position to do so. As it was pointed out, however, some planning with regard to working capital is necessary. Clearly, the company is providing only enough depreciation to take care of the minimum losses in its fixed assets, and is making no provision for obsolescence or other contingencies.

The store of fixed assets owned by an enterprise is not constant. Assets may be disposed of, or additional plant acquired. Furthermore, the diligent management seeks constantly to improve its plant. When there are additions to the assets over and above the replacements, the analyst has more difficulty.

Here, the company has not only replaced the assets which have been written off the books, but has also added considerably to the plant. The reserve was used in the years 1949-1951, inclusive, to the amount of $729,000, but the total deducted from income in the same years was $2,389,000, a sum considerably in excess of the actual retirements. When the value of the plant consistently rises, the annual depreciation should rise in about the same proportion. In this case, a simple calculation shows that the value of the plant increased in 1949 by 10%, in 1950 by 8%, and in 1951 by 6%. In the same years, the annual depreciation increased by 14%, 15%, and 4%, respectively. This increase is probably satisfactory in so far as the increase of assets is concerned.

The question which arises with regard to this company, however, is the reverse of the previous one, in that the annual depreciation charge can be questioned because of its abundance. The total depreciation charged to income for the three years period was $2,839,000. of which only $729,000 was used to retire assets. It would seem that unless there are factors in the type of business that the RST Company conducts which amplify the unpredictable losses, the depreciation charge is excessive. It would appear, therefore, that the profits of the company have been understated, and that the assets are undervalued.

13. *Unwise depreciation policies.* Corporations sometimes pursue certain depreciation policies which the analyst has reason to criticize. A corporation should estimate the depreciation of its fixed assets, and charge a regular depreciation rate which will be sufficient to cover the loss year by year, and enable the assets to be charged off as they are replaced, without affecting cur« rent profits. A policy of setting aside large amounts of depreciation when profits are big, and cutting down the rate when profits decrease, is to be frowned upon. Such a policy neither distributes the loss over the life of the assets, nor gives any assurance that the reserve will be large enough to take care of their retirement.

Another doubtful practice is that of deducting only a part of the depreciation from the income, the remaining portion being charged against surplus. This has the effect of maintaining the depreciation reserve, but, at the same time overstating the annual profits. Except for a policy that omits depreciation altogether, this is probably the one most to be condemned, because the depreciation charge becomes indefinite in amount, and changeable at the whim of the management. Furthermore. that part of the depreciation which is charged against surplus may become hidden in other adjustments, out of sight of anyone but the management.

Corporations which pursue no policy of depreciation present the argument that none is needed because full maintenance of the plant is attained at all times. This argument, of course, is fallacious, as it is impossible to retain indefinitely assets at topmost efficiency, no matter how much they are repaired. Sooner or later, replacement is necessary, and, if no provision has been made by means of a reserve, a heavy loss ensues.

It has become somewhat common practice for corporations to present more favorable profits by reducing the amount of depreciation. This is accomplished by the simple method of writing down the value of the assets against surplus, and, at the same time, reducing the annual depreciation charge. This is a method which the analyst must condemn, because depreciation cannot be eliminated by so simple a means as reducing the book value of the assets. The depreciation still continues despite the fine work of the management, but some day, the piper must be paid.

It is sometimes argued that no criticism should be aimed against a policy which is conservative enough to write down the assets before the end of their lives. This would be sound if the former rates of depreciation were maintained, but the usual course is to reduce the amount of depreciation at the same time. While this eliminates the necessity of charging heavy losses to income at a later date, it does not help to provide means of financing by building up a store of current assets. Profits obtained by the reduction of depreciation are very likely paid in dividends to the stockholders, with a resulting decrease in working capital. Furthermore, when assets are written down prematurely, the balance sheet value does not reflect either their cost or their proper book value.

14. *Depletion defined.* In addition to depreciation, certain types of enterprises must also make allowance for depletion. Whereas depreciation indicates a loss in the value of an asset, depletion indicates that the asset no longer exists. Assets which are subject to depletion are known as "wasting assets," that is, they are used up in the operation of the business. Coal and other products of mines, oil, natural gas, and timber are examples of wasting assets. Companies which own these assets have their regular depreciation problems, but, in addition, they must recognize the fact that part of their fixed assets is being used up with no means of replacement.

If, for instance, a company is organized, with an initial capital of $10,000,000, to cut lumber from timberland, and $8,000,000 of the capital is used to purchase the tract of land, 80% of the stockholders' capital is subject to depletion. Unless capital in the form of current assets is held by the corporation for the stockholders' benefit, or is returned to them as the operations are carried on, they will lose their capital, since nothing will be left at the end but barren land, probably non-saleable. The wasting asset is much like an inventory in that it is used up as the product is manufactured, but it differs from an inventory in that it frequently cannot be replaced. Furthermore, it is a fixed asset and represents most of the permanent capital of the company.

15. *Methods of handling depletion.* Depletion may be handled either as a part of the depreciation charge, or it can be computed and deducted separately from income. Some companies, because of the difficulty of making an accurate computation, Show the deduction after the earnings have been found. Again, some companies frankly omit the depletion charges, in which case the analyst must arbitrarily adjust the earnings of the company by an amount that he estimates is a return of capital, rather than profits. This is extremely difficult inasmuch as the analyst has less data than the management of the company, and his estimate must, therefore, be purely arbitrary.

In almost all cases, an estimate of depletion is at best a guess. It is particularly difficult in the case of mines to arrive at an annual depletion charge. In general, a mining company seeks to determine by engineering methods the expected amount of ore which can profitably be mined. This estimate determines the value of the mine before operations are begun. The estimated value of the mine is then divided by the expected tonnage of the mine, which results in the estimated value per ton. As the ore is extracted, the per ton value is multiplied by the number of tons mined; the result is the approximate depletion. In the case of timber companies, the estimate is not as difficult because timber is visible, and the footage is estimated with more exactness. The value of oil properties is even more difficult than mines.

Inaccuracy in the estimate of the value of the property may have far-reaching effects upon the financial status of the enterprise. If the estimate is too large and the amount of product expected does not materialize, the depletion charges will be too small, the profits will be overstated, and the stockholder will sustain a heavy loss. On the other hand, if the estimates prove to have been too small, the depletion will be too great, and profits will be concealed. In such cases, the stockholder may look for the "cutting of the melon" in the form of extra dividends. In view of all these uncertainties, the analyst is well advised if he overstates rather than understates his estimate of the amount of depletion.

16. *Summary.* The analyst must thus be sure of the following things concerning the depreciation and depletion policy of a company: first, that the company is providing depreciation, and that it is all deducted from the annual income; second, that the depreciation is included in the operating expenses; and third, that the amount is adequate to cover not only the normal replacements of assets, but also the possibility of obsolescence, as well as the further possibility that rising prices may force replacements to be made at higher costs. In the case of wasting assets, the analyst must be sure that some adjustment of profits is made for depletion; otherwise the dividends which the company pays include a return of capital to the stockholder.

Preparation of the Statements for Analysis

1. *Statements need preparation for analysis.* The statements of corporations are rarely so simple that they can be readily analyzed in the form in which they are published. It is usually necessary to prepare them for the analytical process. The extent and kind of preparation which is necessary depends upon the purpose of the analysis. If the analyst merely expects to invest a small sum in the stock of the company, his investigation will not be as "extensive as that made by an investment banker who plans to purchase or underwrite an entire bond issue. By the same token, the analysis for credit purposes will not be as searching as that of the management of a corporation which is about to purchase the entire stock of another enterprise.

The published statements may need adjustment before analysis so that the necessary data are readily available. The balance sheet, for instance, may omit from the current liabilities the amount of the bonds which are due and payable in the subsequent year, in which case the total of the current liabilities is incorrect. Or, as is frequently the case, the depreciation in the income account may be omitted from the operating expenses, thereby causing an overstatement of the profit from operations.

Possibly, treasury stock may be listed as an asset instead of being deducted from the capital stock account. Again, the reserves for depreciation and bad debts may be listed as deferred liabilities, rather than deducted from the assets which they are supposed to revalue. Nothing is very wrong with these methods, but they do not lend themselves to analytical facility.

Furthermore, if the various accounts are large in amount, it is helpful to reinstate them in round numbers so as to make calculations easier. Some analysts favor an entire resetting of the statements so that comparable ac. counts are found together, and believe that time is saved by copying the statements on specially prepared forms which immediately display the desired relationships. In the usual analysis, this procedure is probably not necessary.

2. *Adjusting the statements to round numbers.* Just as it is easier to comprehend the relationship between $100 and $300 than that between $99.78 and $299.98, so also is it easier to realize the relationship between current assets of $8,987,000 and current liabilities of $2,656,000 than that between current assets of $8,986,743.48 and current liabilities of $2,656,199.87. In the first illustration, the cents are insignificant for comparative purposes. In the second illustration, the cents, the dollars, the tens of dollars, and the hundreds of dollars may be discarded without affecting the relationship of the two amounts. It is helpful to restate the statements in terms of round numbers, not only because it simplifies the figures so that their relationship may be understood by inspection, but also because mathematical computations are facilitated, if such are found necessary.

When a statement is revised in round numbers and the hundreds of dollars, for instance, are eliminated, it is usual to add a full thousand dollars when the amount is $500 or over, and drop the amount when it is under $500. Such additions and subtractions, however, may throw the totals out of balance. In order to bring them into balance, it is usual to add or deduct a thousand dollars to or from one of the accounts which has a large balance. Because relationships in general and not in exact dollars are important, this adjustment will ordinarily not affect the analysis.

If the hundreds of dollars are to be eliminated, a problem arises concerning accounts of less than $500. Unless they are of importance, they may be omitted, but if they are of an important nature, they are listed at a thousand dollars. Thus, prepaid insurance of $25 may not be particularly important; but notes receivable of $450 may be too significant to omit because they are part of the current assets which have considerable weight in analysis. In the former case, the amount would be omitted entirely; in the latter case, the account would be listed as $1,000.

From the simplified statements, numerous calculations may be made, either with the aid of a calculating machine or with the ordinary slide rule. If neither of these is available, the amount of work involved in the use of simple arithmetic is not too arduous.

3. *The use of percentage statements.* There is a possibility that the analyst will be influenced in his study of the company statements by the mere size of the figures. The $813,400 cost of sales is likely to be more impressive than the $900 reserve for bad debts. This is particularly true when statements are given a cursory inspection. It is quite possible that for some purposes the latter figure may be the more important. One method of removing the influence of the mere size of figures is to reduce the statements to percentages. This results in what are commonly called 100% statements, or common-size statements, the latter term arising from the fact that, since all such statements are upon the basis of 100%, they are, in fact, common in size. The 100% balance sheet is computed upon the basis of the total assets as 100%, each asset and each liability being a percentage of that total. In the income account, the total of the gross sales is 100% and each other account is a percentage of that amount.

4. *Limitations of analysis for a single year.* Whether the analysis of business statements for a single year is from the original figures, simplified figures, or from percentages, it is statical, and merely shows the proportions of the various accounts which describe the economic elements in the business as of the date of the statements. Such an analysis is thus limited in its scope, but this limitation does not preclude the ability to gain much important information concerning the financial status of the enterprise as of the date of the statements.

5. *Information that can be obtained from the statements of one year.* A business is operating with a high percentage of expenses relative to its income. There is only a 8% margin of sales over expenses to cover a return of profit to the stockholders. This margin can be completely wiped out if the operating expenses are not fully controlled, or if misfortune comes to the company in the form of extraordinary losses. It appears that the cost of sales is too high, indicating that the manufacturing expenses are out of proportion to the total costs.

Turning to the balance sheet; the current assets and their opposing current liabilities appear to be in quite satisfactory proportion. The current assets are 48% of the total assets, and the current liabilities are only 15%. This indicates that there are over $3.00 of current assets for each dollar of current liabilities. The cash appears to be sufficient, but the analyst might question the fact that there are considerable amounts of notes receivable and notes payable. It is quite possible, therefore, that part of the cash balance has been obtained by discounting notes at the bank. If this be true, there are contingent liabilities not mentioned in the balance sheet.

The importance of notes, both receivable and payable, depends upon the credit practices in the trade. If it is the custom to extend credit on notes, the amount may not be open to question; but if such extension is unusual, the analyst may surmise that sales have been made to customers whose credit standing is not entirely satisfactory and from whom notes have been demanded. The notes payable would indicate slow payment of accounts payable, or borrowing.

The investment in fixed assets does not appear to be excessive, representing as it does 50% of the assets, and the distribution between real estate, machinery and equipment, and furniture and fixtures is not unusual. The company is properly depreciating its plant and allowing for uncollectible accounts. Furthermore, it has accumulated a most satisfactory surplus. Consequently, the indications from this very limited analysis are that, contingent upon a reduction in operating expenses and careful management of credit extensions, the company may continue successful operation.

The limitations of the analysis of statements for a single year leads to an investigation of the statements for a series of years in order to obtain better evidence of the results which have been and are being obtained by the management. Dynamic analysis indicates the changes which have taken place in the corporate structure, and seeks to indicate, to some extent, the changes which are likely to occur in the immediate future.

Advisory 5

Preliminary Analysis for a Series of Years

1. *Accounts are subject to constant change.* It has been explained that the values in a business and the rights, or equities, in those values constantly change as operations are carried on. It follows, therefore, that the accounts which represent these values and rights likewise constantly change. The accounts in the balance sheet at the end of a given year differ from those at the end of any other year, and, by the same token, the profit and loss accounts continually change, with the varying results of the operations of the business.

The analyst is keenly interested in these changes because they indicate the manner in which the business is progressing or retrogressing. He compares the company's statements of the current year with those of previous years to learn not only what changes have taken place, but also the acceleration of the changes. A comparison of the current statements with a series of past statements shows him the amount of growth or decline in the various accounts and groups of accounts.

The data thus obtained from a series of trends which are valuable aids in the formation of an opinion as to the true value of the enterprise. Past history is not always an indication of what the future may hold, but a knowledge of past trends is helpful to the analyst at least as a point of departure for speculation as to the future.

2. *A study of trends is necessary for complete analysis.* A thorough method of analysis must measure not only the statements of a single year but also the statements of a series of years.

In no other way can the dynamic results of the enterprise be evaluated. The construction of 100% statements is not completely effective for this purpose. The 100% balance sheet uses the total of the assets as the base for the calculation of the various percentages. Therefore, 100% balance sheets for a series of years are calculated upon different bases. This fact limits their comparability.

The 100% income account uses the sales as the base for its percentages, and a series of such accounts, each calculated upon a different base, is likewise limited in comparability.

The indicated trend of purchases is misleading. The purchases in 1949 as compared with 1948 increased only approximately 6% and not 26% as a cursory glance at the figures would seem to indicate, This exaggeration is caused by the fact that the base upon which the percentage is calculated is $200,000 smaller in 1949 than in 1948. Only by a calculation of the decrease in the sales, together with a calculation of the increase in the purchases, can a logical basis for analysis be found.

3. *Methods of obtaining trend percentages.* Two methods are used in the calculation of trend percentages from a series of statements. The first of these, known as the "chain-percentage method," uses a changing base and, therefore, is to some extent as undesirable as a series of 100% statements. It is briefly described, more as an introduction to the second method—"the base-year method"—than as a recommended method, although it is frequently used.

In the foregoing illustration, the figures are simple and in round numbers so that, by inspection, it may readily be determined that the sales are decreasing and the purchases increasing; certainly not a situation about which the management has occasion to brag. When the figures are more complex, calculations are necessary, and the analyst will want to know not only the amount of the increases or decreases but the rates by which the accounts have changed.

The rate of decrease of the sales on the same basis is 20% in 1949, 12.5% in 1950, and 14.2% in 1951. In the same manner, the purchases show increases of 6.2% in 1949, 5.8% in 1950, and 5.5% in 1951.

As has been pointed out, the base in each calculation changes, which is an undesirable factor. There is, however, another objection to the method. While the figures of each year are compared with those of the previous year, there is no indication as to the status of 1951 as compared with 1949, or with 1948. In other words, a clear trend is not demonstrated.

The above objections are eliminated by the use of the "base-year" method. In this method all the figures of all the years are compared with a common base which results in full comparability, and offers a clear indication of the trend. One problem in the use of this method concerns itself with the choice of the base year. In the foregoing illustration, the year 1948 can be used. This would seem to be logical since it is the first year of the series. It may be contended, however, that 1948 was not a normal year; in which case, all comparisons with it would be abnormal. Some years ago, for instance, the production and sales of a paint manufacturing company were reduced to a minimum by a serious explosion and fire. The statements for that year could not be considered normal. If a given year is abnormal, another year may be used; or if the analyst wishes to use great care, he may accept as a base the average of several years. In general, the base year should bear reasonable similarity to the remaining years of the series; otherwise it may lead to incorrect conclusions.

The base-year percentages are a true trend, whereas the chain-percentages are each dependent upon all the previous figures. The base-year figures show clearly that while the sales were decreasing at the rate of 1000 each year, the purchases were increasing at the rate of only a little over 6% each year. Because the figures in the illustration are simple and in round numbers, the advantage of the base-year method may not be as apparent as if the figures had been more complex.

The usefulness of trend percentages in analysis is great, but they are not without their disadvantages. The use of the percentages rather than the "raw" figures is quite likely to exaggerate small changes in the accounts. Thus, an increase of $100 is 5% of an account with a balance of $2,000, but it is 50% of an account with a balance of $200. On the other hand, the percentages serve to overcome the possibility that accounts with small balances may be disregarded. It is quite possible that a trend in an account having comparatively small balance may be as important as one in an account having a balance of thousands of dollars.

4. *Trend percentages applied to the Eureka Corporation.* The reader will remember that the Eureka Corporation, used as an illustration in the preceding chapter, presented fairly satisfactory financial statements for the year 1949. Only in the amount of operating expenses, and in the large notes receivable and notes payable, were its operations questioned. A study of this corporation for a period of years is now in order to ascertain first, whether its 1949 condition continued: and second, what may be learned from an analysis of its trends.

5. *Statement of differences and percentages for the Eureka Corporation.* It may be brought to the attention of the reader that it is generally not necessary for the analyst to compute all the percentages of changes in the accounts: usually the more important will suffice.

The foregoing complete statement can be used as the basis for a study of the relationships of the component parts of the enterprise. In order to use it intelligently, however, the analyst must have a clear conception of the procedure of a business. He must understand that the owners originally invested funds in fixed and current assets to provide the tools with which the company could produce and ultimately make a profit. He must realize that the amount of funds invested in inventories must remain in that form until the producing process is completed. He must further realize that additional expenditures of capital must be made to cover the labor and manufacturing expenses, and that the product must first reach the finished state before there can be a shift of capital from the manufacturing costs.

The analyst must recognize the shifting in values and the shifting in equities when the product is sold, and either cash is received or credit is extended. Furthermore, he must be prepared to measure the financial result of the time which elapses between the sale and the final receipt of cash. The faster that the cycle, from the purchase of the inventories to the receipt of cash, is completed, the lesser will be the amount of working capital needed. The analyst must give due attention to each of the accounts involved in this cycle. He must also not forget that, as the business process continues, other equities beside the owners' appear, and that there must be a normal amount of velocity in the satisfaction and disappearance of these equities. In other words, liabilities are incurred, and they must be paid without undue tardiness.

The analyst must be aware that there are some very close relationships in the accounts, and he must study these relationships to learn if they are normal or abnormal; and, if the latter be true, what are the causes thereof. The sales, for instance, have a close relationship to the purchases, to the inventories, and to the receivables. The current assets and the current liabilities arise in the main from the same causes, and the whole galaxy of operating expenses is related to the final profit as well as to the sales.

6. *Some methods of analysis are explained.* The statements of the Eureka Corporation will be used to guide the reader through some of the more important analytical relationships which are found in the usual business statements. The reader should be cautioned that the object of the present illustration and explanation is not to give a complete analysis of a business enterprise, but rather to explain a method which can be used together with other tests which are explained in later chapters. The reader may, however, be surprised to learn the extent of the information which may be obtained with ease from a cursory study of a series of business statements.

7. *The sales are studied.* It is quite logical to begin an analysis with the sales of a company. This is the account which shows the results of the operations in terms of the sales of the product, and it is the first account which indicates the way toward the ultimate goal of profit. The gross sales of the Eureka Corporation were $405,000 in 1949, $414,200 in 1950, and $452,500 in 1951. This is an interesting trend which appears all the more satisfactory when placed in percentage form, using 1949 as a base. Increases of 2% in 1950 and 12% in 1951 indicate sales expansion.

It must be remembered, however, that sales are expressed in dollars, and that the figures in the income accounts mean only that the sales account represented more dollars in 1950 and 1951 than in 1949. The question may well be asked: More dollars for what? Do the sales balances mean more dollars because of a greater number of sales, and a greater quantity of the product sold; or do they mean that the same or a lesser amount of the product was sold but at a greater number of dollars per sale. In other words, have the sales increased because of quantity, or because of higher prices?

This distinction is fundamental in the analysis of sales because it is possible for a company, in a period of rapidly rising prices, to have an apparent increase in the number of sales, but actually to sell less goods. In the usual income account and balance sheet, the task of ascertaining what has actually happened is no mean one, for the reason that complete data may not be available. Corporations, because of competition, hesitate to make public complete information concerning their production. In the case of the Eureka Corporation, the analyst is fortunate in having a complete break-down of the various manufacturing expenses including the exact figures for the various inventories.

8. *Accounts that lead to sales analysis.* The various accounts which are closely related to the sales are likely to offer some indication of what has been taking place in the sales account. If more product is being sold, there is likely to be greater activity in the purchases, an increase of inventories, and a greater amount spent for labor and manufacturing expenses. If, on the other hand, the quantity of sales is not increasing, the purchases are likely to show a downward trend, and there may be some indication of slow moving inventories. In such a case, the cost of labor and manufacturing expenses may rise if prices are ascending.

It was noted that the sales of the Eureka Corporation increased in the years 1950 and 1951 by 2% and 12%, respectively. The net purchases amounted to $223,000 in 1949, $217,300 in 1950, and $244,800 in 1951, a decrease of 3% in 1950 as compared with 1949, but an increase of 9% in 1951 as compared with the base year. The slight variations between the purchases and the sales do not warrant any assumption that the purchasing policy is abnormal. A conclusion cannot be reached, however, until attention is given to the various inventories, because the extent of the use of the purchases is reflected in them.

9. *Analysis of the raw material inventories.* It may be assumed that over the three-year period, on the basis of normal purchases, and in view of the increase of sales, there should be no increase of inventories; in fact, it would not be surprising if they showed some decline.

It may further be assumed that, if a lesser amount of the product is being sold, and the purchases are normal, the inventories are likely to show some increase. In checking the inventories, the figure to be used is that which appears in the balance sheet as of the date at which the total sales have been calculated; in this case, December 31.

If the reader studies the inventories of raw materials, bearing in mind the above premises, he may be startled to find that, in 1950, when the sales increased a mere 2% and purchases decreased 3%, the raw materials on hand actually increased 15%. Such an increase might be due to a year-end purchase, to take advantage of a favorable price; but the indications are that such is not the case because, in 1951, when sales increased by 12%, and purchases by 9%, the raw materials again showed an increase of 47%. Despite these large increases of raw materials on hand, the situation might still not be too unsatisfactory, provided that there is a continuous flow through the manufacturing process and into sales. To check upon this flow, the analyst must turn his attention to the inventories of goods in process and finished goods.

10. *Analysis of the goods in process and finished goods inventories.* The goods in process inventory is the amount of raw materials which has been placed in the manufacturing process, and which is still on the machines, or in the stage of being converted into finished goods. If the production at the Eureka Corporation is active, the large raw material inventories should be absorbed in the goods in process inventory in fairly constant amount. It must be noted, however, that while raw materials on hand at the end of December 1950 had increased by 15% over the same date in 1949, the goods in process actually decreased by 30%; and that, in the face of an increase of raw materials at the end of 1951 of 47% over 1949, the goods in process further decreased by 62%. At this point, the analyst should be almost willing to concede that the production of the Eureka Corporation has been decreasing since 1944. He should, however, make other tests.

If production has decreased in 1950 and 1951 despite the increase of the sales balances, the inventory of finished goods should show a proportionate decrease, because the smaller amount added to the inventory of finished goods together with the greater amount deducted from it must have that effect. The contrary appears to be the case. Instead of decreases in the inventory of finished goods, there were increases of 34% and 68% respectively. Finished goods and raw materials have been increasing, therefore, at an alarming rate, a fact which will probably mean depreciation in values and stagnation of working capital.

11. *The indication of the cost of labor.* The analyst may make one more test at this point. Fortunately, he has available the figures for the labor costs over the three-year period. If production has gone down, the result should be a reduction in the amount of wages paid. This seems to be the case, labor costs having decreased by 30% in 1950 and by 58% in 1951, decreases that are too large to be the result of reductions in wage fates.

The analyst should now be fairly sure that there has been a large decrease in production, and that the increase in sales must have come about through an increase in prices. No doubt he is puzzled by the fact that the company has shown an increasing profit. He must realize, however, that this increase has come about very largely through the lower labor cost. The question arises as to whether the more favorable profit can be counted upon for the future, or whether it is merely temporary and subject to reversal as inventory losses and credit train become acute.

The lower labor cost has undoubtedly come from lesser employment of workers, because it does not seem logical that the company could cut its wage rates and, at the same time, increase the price of its commodity. The possibility that the company has found a cheaper method of production, possibly by the introduction of new types of machines, cannot be ignored; but this possibility does not explain the piling up of inventories. The analyst is forced to come to the conclusion that the inventory situation is very unsatisfactory; and he turns his attention, for the time being, to other accounts.

12. *Credit position of the Eureka Corporation.* Inasmuch as purchases, to some extent, result in accounts payable, and sales result in accounts receivable, an investigation of these two important accounts is next in order. If the credit department of a business is properly functioning, the accounts receivable should not increase at a greater rate than the sales; and, by the same token, the accounts payable should not run ahead of the purchases. A comparison of the accounts receivable with the sales, and the accounts payable with the purchases, therefore, gives some indication as to the collection policy of an enterprise and whether it pays its bills promptly or is tardy in the settlement of its liabilities.

It has already been noted that the purchases decreased in 1950 by 8% and increased in 1951 by 9%. Consequently, no large increase in accounts payable should be anticipated. The analyst finds that the situation in accounts payable is not entirely satisfactory because they increased in 1950 and 1951 by 17% and 33%, respectively. This, however, may not be the whole story because, in addition to the accounts payable, there has been, in the same years, an increase in notes payable of 384% and 277%. At first thought, this might seem astonishing, but the analyst cannot assume that such large increases in notes were due entirely to unpaid purchases; the amounts are far too large. In order to be sure, he must forsake his percentages, and refer to the original balance sheets and income accounts.

The purchases in 1950 amounted to $217,300, after the deduction of discounts. It is not reasonable to assume that, of this total, as much as $52,700 accounts payable and $69,000 notes payable would still be owed.

Creditors do not continue to extend credit under such conditions. Therefore, the notes payable must, in part, have resulted from some other type of transaction. The analyst makes a memorandum of this for further investigation.

He now turns to the accounts and notes receivable. Here, he finds that whereas the accounts receivable increased in 1950 and 1951 by 63% and 76%, the sales increased in the same years by only 2% and 12%. In addition, the balance of the notes receivable account has constantly increased, and by amounts which seem to indicate that the increases were due to notes received from customers in settlement of past-due accounts. The disparity between the accounts and notes receivable and the sales raises the question as to whether some of the increase in sales, at least in 1950, was not made at the expense of selling to poor risks. If such is the case, the company must safeguard itself against heavy future losses by a proper provision from profits of a reserve for bad debts.

13. **The reserve for bad debts.** The analyst notes that the company has set aside from profits in each year an amount to provide against losses from uncollectible accounts. The amount of the reserve deducted in the income accounts was $900 in 1949, and $800 in 1950 and 1951. It is possible that the analyst may not know the usual experience with bad debts which businesses of the type of the Eureka Corporation have had, but he may assume that about 2% or 3% of the outstanding accounts receivable at the end of each year would be a fair estimate under ordinary conditions. A calculation shows that 3% of the outstanding accounts receivable amounts to $1,820 in 1949, $2,145 in 1950, and $2,822 in 1951. Thus, in the three years, the company, on the basis of a fair estimate, should have set aside from its profits a total of $5,787, but it actually provided only $2,500. This is entirely inadequate; particularly in View of the growth of outstanding accounts as shown by the previous analysis. If the notes receivable are included, the annual deduction from profits should have been $1,985 in 1949, $2,955 in 1950, and $3,267 in 1951; Or $5,657 more than was provided.

A check of the experience of the company over the three-year period adds to the evidence. The balance of the reserve for bad debts in the 1949 balance sheet was $8,800. In 1950, the company added $800 from its profits so that the total reserve at the end of 1950 should be $4,100, provided no use was made of the reserve. An inspection of the 1950 balance shows that this was the balance. The company, therefore, used no part of the reserve in that year.

Applying the same procedure to the reserve for the next year, however, the fact is revealed that the balance of the reserve should have been $4,900 (1950 balance of $4,100 plus the amount reserved from the 1951 profits of $800). The balance on December 31, 1951, however, was only $2,600. Thus, $2,300 was deducted during the year. The assumption of the analyst, that the reserve is inadequate, appears to be valid because, in one year, the losses from bad debts were nearly as great as the provision for the entire three-year period. The analyst, for his future use, makes note of the amount by which the reserve should have been increased.

14. **What the discounts show.** There now seems to be conclusive evidence of the slowness of the accounts receivable, and the tardiness of the company in paying its current liabilities. If the analyst wishes additional evidence, he can analyze the discount on purchases and the discount on sales. The discount on purchases in 1950 decreased 15%, when purchases decreased only 3%; and, in the following year, when purchases increased by 9%, the discount on purchases

decreased 30%. Likewise, the discount on sales in 1950 was lower by 38% than in 1949, at a time when sales increased by 2%; and, in 1951, the discount on sales decreased 50%, in the face of an increase of sales of 12%. The slowness of the payables and the receivables is reflected in the fewer discounts taken, and the analyst is now able to make an addition to his assumption that the credit policy of the Eureka Corporation is extremely poor and that large losses from bad debts may be anticipated.

15. *Analysis of the fixed assets.* Attention may now be turned from the current assets to the fixed assets. Heavy increases during the three-year period will probably be noticed immediately; real estate by $40,000, machinery and equipment by $50,000, and furniture and fixtures by $35,000. In addition, the securities owned which are listed among the fixed assets have also increased by $15,000. It is quite evident that a major transaction took place in 1950. The analyst is interested in two phases of this transaction; first, the increases in the asset accounts, and second, the manner in which the increases came about or were financed.

The inclusion of good will in the fixed assets may cause comment because it is usually listed as a deferred asset. It is considered with the fixed assets, in this instance, because it seems to have some relationship to the general rise in fixed values. By the same token, the securities owned may be eliminated from the increases in the fixed asset accounts, because a close relationship seems to be lacking.

In order to find some indication as to the sources from which these assets came, the analyst has recourse to the rules governing the changes in the accounting equation. (The classification of changes in values in the accounting equation was stated in Chapter 2.) The analyst knows that assets can increase from three sources only; by means of decreases in other asset accounts, by increases of liabilities, or by increases of proprietorship (capital).

16. *Application of the rule governing increases of assets.* Applying the rule, the analyst checks the various asset accounts for decreases which might give him a clue. The only decrease appears in the goods in process inventory which has no relationship to the fixed asset accounts, and, furthermore, could not be a source of capital funds inasmuch as an inventory in an unfinished state is not readily saleable. The increases in the fixed accounts cannot be explained, therefore, by decreases in other asset accounts. The analyst must proceed to investigate the liabilities.

Here, the analyst has more evidence. A mortgage appears for the first time in 1950. This is probably upon the total land and buildings owned at the end of that year. The analyst also remembers that the Notes Payable increased by $53,100 in that year, and he had decided the amount was too large to have resulted from the payment of accounts payable.

He now believes that most of this increase was in connection with the acquisition of the plant items. What the distribution may be between notes given in payment for purchases and those due to banks, or to the vendors of the plant, cannot be ascertained from the data which are available. The analyst must depend upon his estimate. The increase in the accounts payable, while greater than good credit procedure would permit, nevertheless is probably due to ordinary business operations.

The capital stock section of the balance sheet reveals an adjustment in the treasury stock. Treasury stock is capital stock of a company which, having been originally issued, has been reacquired by the company. It can be retired, and the capital stock reduced accordingly, or it can be held for reissue or sale. In 1950, the treasury stock decreased by $35,000, but the capital stock account remained at its former balance. The treasury stock was therefore reissued. Whether it was sold and the proceeds used in payment of the additional plant, or whether it was transferred directly to the vendors of the plant makes no difference. In either case, it clearly would have a relation to the transaction the analyst is now investigating.

The surplus account of a company should always be checked, because adjustments are frequently made directly through surplus, rather than through the income account. Accountants frown upon such adjustments, but they are still made despite good accounting procedure. The balance of the surplus account at the end of 1949 was $84,100, and the income account for 1950 showed a net profit of $37,300. The total surplus at the end of 1950, therefore, should be the total of these two figures, or $121,400. The analyst finds that the balance sheet for 1950 shows the surplus as $146,400. There is thus a discrepancy of $25,000 between the two amounts. The surplus account has been increased by this amount from some other source than through the profits as shown by the income account. The analyst assumes that this adjustment also relates to the acquisition of plant.

The sum of $8,000 is still unaccounted for, and the analyst reasons that the capital surplus account originally contained an amount of $7,300 which was transferred to a reserve for contingencies in 1950, and so stated on the balance sheet. While it is not possible to check a transaction such as this, dollar for dollar, the estimates made by the analyst are close enough to warrant the assumption that they are in the main correct.

Unless further data are available, the analyst may rest upon an assumption that the Eureka Corporation purchased the assets of another company; paying some $25,000 more than the former book value, and giving in payment a variety of liabilities. He may wonder, however, what part these assets played in the increase of profit in 1950 and 1951. Certainly, something was responsible for the reduction in labor costs, a reduction which was large, even if full account is taken of the undoubted decrease in production.

If the assets acquired were responsible for some of the decrease in costs, the analyst may have no desire to criticize their acquisition; he may have reason, however, to question the method by which they were acquired. The increase in current liabilities, together with the assumption of a long-term mortgage, and the inclusion of doubtful good will, would not appear to be the best method of financing permanent assets, particularly when there is good reason to believe that they are overvalued.

17. *The depreciation policy.* The question of the valuation of the fixed assets leads the analyst to a study of the depreciation policy of the Eureka Corporation. He notes that in each year an amount has been reserved from the profits to cover depreciation. Since the depreciation is stated in a single figure, he must depend upon an assumption to provide a break-down of the charges against the individual fixed assets. Furthermore, the real estate account includes both land and buildings, and land does not depreciate in the usual meaning of the word. Land values fluctuate but do not disappear through wear and tear as do values of other fixed assets, such as buildings or machinery.

The analyst estimates that the value of the land might be somewhere between thirty and forty per cent of the total value of the real estate. Therefore, he deducts $50,000 from the book value of the real estate in 1949 and $65,000 from the book value of the real estate in 1950 and 1951 in order to obtain the estimated value of the buildings. The depreciable value of the buildings would then be $85,000 in 1949, and $110,000 in 1950 and 1951.

If the estimates of the analyst have been fair, the company, over a period of three years, should have set aside $45,250, or over 50% of its total profits; whereas it provided only $9,000. The management of the company may argue that, inasmuch as none of the fixed assets had to be replaced during the period, its estimates are sufficient. This argument is not valid when the long-term situation of the company is considered, because sooner or later replacements will have to be made. If the reserves are not adequate, the entire losses will have to be deducted from the profits in one year: a situation which will be unfortunate for the stockholders.

18. *The 1951 Surplus Account.* The analyst has checked the 1950 surplus account, and has found that it had been inflated by $25,000, probably by a write-up of fixed assets. Thus far, he has had no occasion to check the 1951 surplus account. This he proceeds to do. The balance of the surplus as shown by the 1950 balance sheet was $146,400. The profit shown by the 1951 income account was $35,700. The total surplus, before dividends, therefore, should be $182,100. Dividends were paid in 1951, amounting to $17,100. Deducting this amount from the $182,100 gives $165,000 as the balance of surplus which should appear in the 1951 balance sheet. Again, in 1951, there is a discrepancy, because the balance sheet shows a surplus balance of $185,000, or $20,000 more than the income account indicated. There is no positive method

of proving how this discrepancy came about, but the company's method in 1950 causes at least a suspicion that the $20,000 increase in machinery and equipment may correspond with the increase of the surplus, in which case an outright inflation in values is indicated. The analyst makes note of this as a possible inflation in value.

19. **The analyst's adjustment of the Eureka Corporation surplus.** The analyst believes that his adjustment for deterioration of inventories is fair; in fact, he believes that the eventual loss, if they are not moved faster, may be much greater. The balance of the adjustments is the result of his previous calculations, and he also believes them to be fair. He therefore arrives at a final balance of surplus of $24,463 as compared with $185,000 as shown by the balance sheet. He cannot fail to consider that his adjusted surplus is offset by good will of $30,000, which may or may not be valuable, and he fears it may not be worth very much. Therefore, the company surplus is almost non-existent, and the analyst can have no good opinion of the Eureka Corporation.

The foregoing illustrations are sufficient to demonstrate the manner in which information may be obtained concerning the operations of a company, and to demonstrate a method by which financial data may be analyzed. Additional tests will be explained in the chapters which follow.

Advisory 6

Analysis of Earnings

1. *The analysis of earnings.* The earnings of an enterprise need more analysis than a mere testing of their sufficiency. Although the current earnings, as shown by the income account, have a considerable effect upon the attitude of the analyst toward the financial standing of the enterprise, and although they also have considerable effect upon the prices of its securities in the stock market, nevertheless, the earnings must be studied intensively, since they cannot always be taken at their face value.

2. *Earnings may he considered from three viewpoints.* Current earnings, good or poor, may be the result of quite temporary conditions in the enterprise, and, if the analyst disregards entirely their past history, he may arrive at an erroneous conclusion. One problem before the analyst, therefore, relates to the study of the current earnings in connection with those of previous years. He may compare the current profits per share with the average for a number of past years, and be quite satisfied that the current earnings are adequate in view of those of the past. On the other hand, a study of the past earnings may result in quite the opposite conclusion with regard to the current profits.

At the same time, the analyst must not neglect the trend of earnings which may give some indication of their future possibilities. In short, the analyst must consider earnings from three viewpoints; those of the current year, the average for a number of years in the past, and the trend which they have displayed.

3. *Adequate earnings are essential.* In order to pass muster, the enterprise must, of course, show sufficient earnings to warrant either additional contributions of capital funds, or at least the retention of capital in the enterprise. The amount of earnings which is satisfactory is dependent upon the type of the enterprise, and upon the purpose of the person, or persons, for whom the analysis is being made.

If the enterprise is in an industry which usually has great stability of earnings, a fair annual rate of return upon the invested capital may be considered sufficient. This rate of return may include no great amount to cover extraordinary risk. If, however, the industry is one in which production and its resulting profits vary widely from year to year, the rate of return which is expected by the owners will be much larger, in order to provide sufficient earnings in good years so that part of these earnings may be carried over to meet dividends in years when profits are lower. Such an enterprise may show quite sufficient current earnings, a satisfactory average, but frequently an unsatisfactory trend.

The purpose for which the analysis is being made likewise has its effect upon the question of the sufficiency of the profits. If the analysis is being made to determine the worth of the corporate securities from the standpoint of long-term investment value, the earnings must be satisfactory from all three viewpoints; the current, the average, and the trend. If, however, the analysis is being made for one who wishes to trade in the stock market on a short-term speculative basis, the current earnings and trend of earnings will probably be emphasized, and little attention paid to the average.

4. *The sufficiency of earnings frequently determined by the capital market.* Some writers contend that sufficient profits exist only when an enterprise is able to produce and sell every unit possible, consistent with the capital invested in plant. This goal is usually too high for the average enterprise, and would cause too large a proportion of all companies to be regarded as financially unsatisfactory. A more logical contention is that an enterprise which is able to earn enough to give to its owners a fair return upon their investment, and, at the same time, retain enough profits to take care of future contingencies, is satisfactory from the profit-making standpoint.

Thus, if a dividend of 5% upon the par value of the capital stock is paid to the stockholders of an enterprise, and if, at the same time, some earnings have been retained in the surplus account for purposes of financial safety, and if, in addition, the 5% dividend is sufficient to encourage investors to retain their capital in the enterprise, the earnings are satisfactory. This does not preclude the possibility that, if the earnings should rise, 1% higher dividend and an increase in price for the capital stock may be indicated.

5. *The earnings should be recurring.* The analyst must determine whether the current earnings are normal, or whether they are merely the result of a non-recurring financial

condition. If the latter is true, the analyst must seek the cause or causes for such abnormality. Abnormal earnings may be the result of factors within the enterprise, or they may be the consequence of conditions which have affected the industry as a whole. If it appears that the trouble is within the enterprise, the analyst must examine the financial statements with great care, and, by means of the various tests which have already been described, try to learn the exact reason or reasons. If the abnormal earnings have not come about because of factors within the company, a study of the statements of a few similar companies is likely to reveal their widespread occurrence in the industry.

6. *Care is necessary in averaging earnings.* The average earnings for a period of years is an important figure, but care must be used in the calculation, so that a true average is obtained, because an average absorbs the minor fluctuations of yearly profits. That which was stated in an earlier chapter concerning the preparation of standard figures is also applicable to the computation of average earnings. Each of the figures included in the average must bear some resemblance in size. If the earnings of one or more of the years in question are out of proportion to the remaining figures, such year or years should be omitted as being of an extraordinary nature. In cases where earnings have fluctuated violently, and deficits appear, the average is of doubtful value, and the analyst will make little use of the figure except to note the fact and mark it down as an unsatisfactory indication.

7. *The trend of earnings is merely an indication, not a prediction.* The trend of earnings is a satisfactory indication of what the enterprise has been able to do in the past. Considered by itself, however, too much emphasis cannot be placed upon it. It is, at best, merely collateral evidence that the earnings have formed themselves into a rising or a falling pattern. The analyst will be favorably disposed in the case of the former, and will exercise more scrutiny in the case of the latter. As an indication for the future, the trend cannot be depended upon, because it may quickly turn. When other financial factors shown by the statements of an enterprise offer a preponderance of evidence, either positively or negatively conclusive, the analyst may decide to place some dependence upon a significant trend as an indication of the future.

8. *The average and the trend must be calculated over a considerable time.* A study of the average and of the trend of earnings should include a considerable number of years. Not only do minor fluctuations appear from year to year, but changes occur as a result of the business cycle in its swing from prosperity to depression and vice versa. The period to be studied must be sufficiently long, therefore, to absorb all of the minor changes, and go be not greatly affected by the major changes. Much dependence cannot be placed upon the history of earnings for a period shorter than ten years, and, in instances where major upheavals have taken place, a period of fifteen years may not be too long. The longer the period studied, the less likely will be the probability of error.

9. *Earnings and the dividend rate.* The earnings of an enterprise must be studied in their relation to the dividend rate and in relation to the market prices of the securities which have been issued. Favorable and unfavorable earnings are reflected in the price of the stock in the market. While the market prices are conditioned to a considerable extent by the dividend rate, they are also affected by the current earnings per share, and, to a lesser extent, by the average earnings per share.

The analyst must observe the dividend rate; both that currently paid, and the rates of past years. The dividend rate is now commonly stated as a number of dollars per share rather than as a percentage of the par value of the capital stock. This method is used because of the large number of no par stocks, upon which the dividend must be quoted in dollars.

The dividend rate for a period of years indicates the agreeableness or the reluctance of the directors to distribute profits to the shareholders, and it is an important factor in the analysis of market prices. Managements generally fix a regular dividend rate which they anticipate will be adequately covered by the profits, not only in the average year, but also in years when the profits may be abnormally low. If, in a given year, the profits exceed the average, the distribution may include an extra dividend. The extra dividend signifies a temporary action, and it is not to be regarded as an increase in the regular dividend rate. The analyst checks the actions of the management in such years because, if extra dividends have been the rule, rather than the exception, the market price of the common stock is governed to a greater extent by the earnings per share than by the regular dividend rate.

10. *The analyst's estimate of a fair price for the common stock.* The average profits per share and the dividend rate enable the analyst to make a rough estimate of the fair market price of the common stock. Allowance in this estimate must be made for the result of the analyst's investigation of the statements of the enterprise. Thus, where the balance sheet and income account clearly demonstrate that the enterprise is overtrading, and is weak in working capital, the estimated value of its common stock should not be entirely determined by the average of its per-share earnings and its dividend rate. The analyst must deduct something from his estimate to allow for possible imminent financial difficulty. By the same token. the analyst adds something to his estimated value of a common stock when his investigation of the company's financial position reveals elements of great strength.

11. *The purchaser's rate of return.* The analyst may also make a rough estimate of the value of a common stock upon the basis of the rate of return demanded by purchasers of securities of similar type. Thus, if the usual rate of return which attracts purchasers is 4%, a share of stock which carries a dividend of 4%, other things being equal, should sell at approximately $100 per share. The purchaser, however, may not be willing to pay $100 for the stock if the $4 dividend uses up all the earnings, because he may realize that nothing has been set aside to act

as a back-log for future dividend payments. The amount of earnings which should be "plowed back" in the business depends upon the degree of risk in the particular type of enterprise. If there is little stability of earnings, a larger amount is necessary than if the earnings will, under normal circumstances, be fairly constant from year to year. If the current earnings are not sufficient to meet the purchaser's requirements, he will only be willing to pay a price which is much less than $100 per share.

When the dividend rate is larger than $4 per share, the purchaser in a 4% market will ordinarily pay a price which will yield him approximately that amount. Thus, if the dividend rate is $6 per share and the average return on stock purchases is 4%, the purchaser may be willing to pay a maximum of $150 per share, because a dividend of $6 would yield him 4% on that amount. Whether he will be willing to pay more or less than this amount depends upon the possibilities of the future, the strength of the company, its standing in the industry; and the attitude of the market.

If the dividend rate is lower than $4, and the average market yield is 4%, the purchaser usually will not be willing to pay as much as $100 for his shares. At a dividend rate of $3, the purchaser may be willing to pay only approximately $75 per share, a price which will give him the market yield.

12. *Other factors enter into market prices.* It must be hastily remarked that the foregoing calculations are mathematical only, and do not take into consideration the prices which may be paid on a speculative basis. In such cases, return upon capital is only a secondary factor. Furthermore, it is not to be supposed that every stock which carries a dividend of $3 per share will sell around $75 under the conditions named above; nor will every stock that has a dividend of $4, under the same conditions, sell in the neighborhood of $100 per share. Many factors affect the determination of the market price.

The general economic condition of the country, the political prospect, the supply of and the demand for the product, the general reputation of the enterprise, and technical stock market situations all enter into the determination of market prices of securities. In addition, the amount of the particular stock which is available for purchase, and the demand of purchasers, enter into its market value. Some of these factors are brought to light by a detailed analysis of the enterprise, but others are in the realm of security analysis, a type of analysis which is not included in the subject matter of these pages.

The analyst, after a searching investigation of the financial situation of an enterprise, and after an examination of the book value per share, as well as the current asset value per share of the capital stock, can arrive at a conclusion that the current market price is either too high or too low. He will then look for additional factors, got yet included in his investigation, which may show the reasons for the lack of adjustment between the estimated value of the stock and its market price.

13. ***Analysis of a preferred stock is also necessary.*** Thus far, the discussion of earnings has been entirely from the standpoint of common stock. No mention has been made of the problem of the sufficiency of earnings when prior claims, such as preferred stock or bonds, exist. In view of the fact that the preferred stock is entitled to a certain fixed and limited return, it would seem that the analyst could solve the problem by merely deducting the preferred dividend from the earnings, prior to his calculation of the rate of return upon the common stock.

This problem, however, cannot be so easily dismissed. The analyst may be making his investigation on behalf of a proposed commitment in preferred stock, in which case, the whole analytical process will be pointed toward that issue. But, when the analysis from the standpoint of the common stock, it must be remembered that the common stock has no claim to the earnings until the dividend upon the preferred stock has been paid. Therefore, an analysis of the position of the preferred stock is necessary in either of the above instances.

14. ***Analysis of the interest on bonds is likewise necessary.*** The position of the interest on bonds in the financial data is also of consequence in analysis. It is true that the interest on bonds is deducted from the profit from operations before the final profit is calculated, but the earnings available for the preferred stock as well as for the common stock are dependent upon the payment of this interest, and anything which causes even the slightest doubt about its payment affects the standing of all the issues of stocks.

15. ***The ratio of earnings to interest charges.*** The ratio of earnings to interest charges is the test which is usually applied on behalf of the bonds. This ratio indicates the number of times the interest charges have been earned. The higher this ratio, the greater is the safety of the periodic interest payments of the bonds. The ratio does not test the probability of the payment of the principal of the bonds; this is dependent upon the general financial position of the enterprise, and is a problem for the future.

If there is only one bond issue, the calculation of the ratio is a simple matter, because only one interest payment need be considered. If there are two or more bond issues, the calculation becomes more complicated because each of the issues must be tested separately, in addition to the interest charges as a whole. The proportion of the earnings used for each issue of bonds varies with the amount of the bonds and the interest rate. Therefore, the interest coverage (the ratio of earnings to interest charges) may vary for each issue of bonds.

Moreover, it is fair to state that the coverage for all the issues must be adequate, or they all must be considered unsatisfactory investments. If, for instance, there is doubt as to the payment of the interest upon an issue of junior bonds, that is, second mortgage bonds, or debenture bonds, the senior securities (the mortgage bonds), will be affected, because, in the event of a default, insolvency or a receivership may follow.

16. *Extraordinary charges and credits are not included in the earnings.* The earnings figure used in the calculation of the ratio of earnings to interest charges is the amount available for the payment of these charges. This ordinarily is the earnings figure after the deduction of taxes and any other fixed charges, not including the interest. Care should be exercised that non-recurrent items are eliminated from the earnings figure. While it is undoubtedly true that extraordinary profits may be used for the payment of fixed charges; nevertheless, they cannot be counted upon as a source of earnings in later periods, and their inclusion in calculation of interest coverage is likely to result in a false premise for future years. In like manner, extraordinary losses may, in a particular year, cut down the interest coverage; but, since it is not to be assumed that they will recur, they should also be eliminated from the ratio.

As previously stated, all the bond issues of an enterprise are affected adversely if there is a default in the interest of any one of them. Because of this fact, some writers have insisted that all issues have the same coverage. This coverage is calculated by dividing the total earnings available for fixed charges by the sum of all the interest charges. Under this theory, both the mortgage bonds and the debenture bonds would be covered 2.15 times. While there is much to be said for this method, it would seem, in many instances, to be somewhat drastic, and the previous method is advocated for general use.

17. *Stability of earnings varies in different types of enterprises.* When the question of a satisfactory ratio of earnings to interest charges is considered, it must be remembered that this ratio is a purely quantitative one, and as such, will not vary in different enterprises to the same extent as some of the other ratios which have been discussed. The earnings of some types of enterprises, however, are subject to greater fluctuation than others. The chief reason lies in the fact that some types of industries are accustomed to having a steady flow of income, while others receive their revenue sporadically. Enterprises which, because of their type of business, receive their income without great variation from month to month, and year to year, are in a much better position to pay their fixed charges than those which have a varying flow of income.

On this score, and for purposes of general analysis, enterprises may be placed in three classes: the public utility operating companies, the railroads, and the industrials. Generally, the public utility operating companies have the most steady flow of revenue. This is due in part to the fact that they render a necessary service, and in part to the fact that they have a monopoly. They also are the least affected by the normal operation of the business cycle.

The railroads also have a comparatively steady flow of revenue, operate as monopolies, and render a necessary service. The railroads, however, are affected to a much greater extent by fluctuations in business. Furthermore, they have large quantities of debt, a fact which makes them more vulnerable when earnings decrease. The industrials, except for those which are well established, and a few which are to some extent depression-proof, are subject to wide fluctuations of earnings. They are entirely dependent upon general business conditions and, in addition, are subject to competition.

18. *Standard ratios of earnings to fixed charges.* Because of the difference in the stability of income in these three types of industries, a different quantitative standard for interest coverage must be used for each. Numerous norms have been established by various writers who have their individual reasons for their suggestions. Some of these norms are much more stringent than others.

Whether the average minimum coverage, in accordance with this schedule, is satisfactory to the analyst, or whether he desires a more stringent standard, depends upon the state of the particular industry at the time the test is made, and upon the opinion which the analyst has formed of the particular company as a result of his analysis. Again, the purpose of the analysis is important because the analyst may be inclined to shade the earnings requirement if the objective be that of a speculative commitment, and to hold strictly to the standard if it be one of investment.

The minimum coverage should have been maintained by the enterprise for a period of at least five years, if the bonds have been that long outstanding. If the issue is new, the analyst calculates the ratio on the basis of the current interest obligations and the earnings for each of the previous five years. If the average coverage is only slightly below the minimum, the analyst is guided by other elements of strength and weakness in the enterprise. In some instances, he may decide that a very favorable current financial situation is sufficient to overcome the lack of sucffient coverage in the past.

19. *Coverage of preferred stock dividends.* After the payment of the fixed charges, the balance of the earnings is available for dividends. If there is preferred stock, the directors of the enterprise determine whether it is to receive a dividend. Because the payment of preferred dividends is entirely in the hands of the directors, assurance of its payment comes only when the earnings are large enough to raise no doubt in their minds as to the advisability of its payment. The preferred stockholders, therefore, are particularly interested in the extent of the coverage of their dividend. Not only do they want to be sure that all prior obligations have been fully covered, but they also want to be sure that the earnings are sufficient to pay them dividends beyond the peradventure of a doubt. Consequently, a quantitative test must be set up for the preferred stock.

The preferred stockholders should expect that all prior obligations will have been covered by earnings at least of the same amount as that required for an investment commitment in the bonds. In addition, they should expect that the full payment of their dividend be satisfactorily covered by earnings. In cases in which there is great risk, they may even expect earnings in addition to the minimum requirements.

As in the case of the ratio of earnings to interest charges, this ratio should be taken for at least a five-year period if the preferred stock has been in existence that long. If not, the past earnings may be applied to the current interest and dividends, with the necessary adjustments for capital changes that have occurred.

20. *Fixed charge and dividend coverage may be the first step in analysis.* If the analysis of an enterprise is being made solely for the purpose of determining the advisability of a purchase of securities in the stock market, it is quite possible that the analyst will make the tests outlined in this chapter at the beginning of his investigation. The earnings factor is paramount in such analysis, and, if it should be determined at the outset that the enterprise lacks the earning power necessary for the maintenance of market value, there would be little need of proceeding further. If, on the other hand, the earning power seems to be satisfactory, or at least passable, additional investigation is in order. When analyses are made for other purposes, the examination of the earnings may come at any point in the analytical process.

Advisory 7

A Comprehensive Problem in Analysis

1. *Preface to the problem.* The student of financial analysis will find that the most satisfactory method of learning how to use the analytical process is to apply the information which he has obtained from the foregoing chapters to specific data. He will discover that mastery of the subject can only be obtained by performance; that the mere reading of descriptions is inadequate.

With this in mind, the following financial data have been prepared for those who wish to apply their knowledge of analysis. The data are as complete as will ordinarily be available to the prospective purchaser of securities. Some additional data are supplied, however, in order to give the reader the full advantage of that which, in the normal course of events, would require some research upon his part. Furthermore, a fairly exhaustive, but not complete, guide to the analysis of the data is furnished.

It is suggested that, as the data are analyzed, the reader review the text material in the previous chapters; page notations are made available for this purpose.

The problem is based upon a company which manufactures and sells cigarettes. This industry has been chosen because it is well-established, because there is a constant demand for its product, and because it is reasonably stable.

2. *How tobacco is grown.* As a preliminary to the problem, the following brief facts concerning the tobacco business may be found helpful. Tobacco is a crop which requires careful farming. It is not a crop which can be sown with little preparation, nor one which can be grown with little care. The soil in which the tobacco seeds are planted must be carefully prepared and well burned over to make it as sterile as possible. It must have a liberal application of fertilizer, usually about 800 pounds to the acre. The result of proper preparation and fertilization is an average yield of about 1,000 pounds of tobacco per acre. Furthermore, the sowing of the seed is a particularly delicate operation, inasmuch as one teaspoonful will sow between 6 and 7 acres.

When the tobacco crop has matured, the leaves are picked and tied in bunches. They are then exposed to heat in curing barns. Ordinarily, the fresh leaves require a steady heat over a period of four days and nights, after which, the bunches of tobacco are hung on rods, covered with canvas, and taken by truck to the market.

3. *The manufacture of cigarettes.* When the dried tobacco leaves are received by the manufacturer, they are put through a vacuum process to remove dirt and loose stalks. They are then remoistened, after which, the leaves are stripped. The stripping process removes the stems and rough material. Following the stripping, the tobacco is packed in hogsheads for further conditioning and later blending. After the proper blend has been attained, the tobacco, in the case of cigarette manufacturers, is shredded in cutting machines. The cigarettes are finally processed, intricate machinery being used so that the tobacco is not touched by the human hand from the time it enters the process until the final purchaser opens the package.

The manufacturing process covers a period of from two to four years, depending upon the type of product which is to be manufactured. Since the process takes so long, the carrying charges are necessarily heavy. Inventories, being large, must be financed, and bank credit is used to a considerable extent by some companies. Because the inventories are held for a period of several years, it is usual to price the raw material at an average of three years' cost.

4. *The financial position of the tobacco industry.* The prices of leaf tobacco usually rise and fall more rapidly than the prices of the manufactured product. When the national income rises, the tendency of raw tobacco prices is to increase; when the national income falls, the opposite tendency ensues. The tobacco manufacturer, in normal times, is usually able to offset these fluctuations by small price adjustments, thereby maintaining stable earnings. This was not true during the period of price control, but such a period is not contemplated in the present problem.

The industry, because of the rising demand for its products, has been in a relatively fortunate position. It was one of the last to feel the effect of the depression in the 1930's, and, to date, there is no indication of any decrease in the demand for its products.

Among the larger manufacturers, competition is keen and advertising expenditures are large. The chief problem of the industry seems to be the adequate financing of its large capital investment in inventories.

5. *History of the company.* This company has been continuously operating since its incorporation in the State of Virginia in 1900. Its products include several popular brands of cigarettes, as well as several brands of cigars and smoking tobacco. It produces a small quantity of chewing tobacco.

The company owns 85% of the $675,000 capital stock of the United States Package Corporation, of Philadelphia, which manufactures packages, cartons, and tins. The company's manufacturing plants are found in six localities in Virginia, Kentucky, and Maryland; and its warehouses are situated near all the leading tobacco centers.

6. *The bonds.* The 4% debenture bonds are subject to a yearly sinking fund of $100,000, which the trustee must apply to their purchase and retirement. If, however, he is unable to purchase bonds at a price of 110, or less, he must return the remaining balance of the sinking fund installment to the corporation.

The issue is non-callable and is a direct obligation of the company, but is secured by no lien or mortgage. The company covenants, however, that no mortgage will be placed upon the property in the future, except subject to the prior lien of these bonds. The company agrees to pay the federal income tax up to the amount of 2%. In addition, this issue has a prior claim upon the assets of the company over the 8% debenture issue which it antedates.

The average prices of the bonds were: Year A, 108; Year B, 110; Year G, 115; Year D, 112; and Year E, 109. The 3% debenture bonds are similar in all details to the 4% issue, but subject to the prior lien of the latter. The average prices were: Year A, 103; Year B, 106; Year C, 110; Year D, 106; Year E, 103.

7. *The preferred stock.* This stock has preference as to assets and as to cumulative dividends at the rate of 7% Per annum. In liquidation, it is entitled to par and accrued dividends. It is non-callable. The preferred stock and the common stock have equal voting rights.

8. *Stock prices.* The average prices for the preferred stock were: Year A, 107; Year B, 117; Year C, 125; Year D, 120; Year E, 115.

The average prices for the common stock were: Year A, 15; Year B, 18; Year G, 20; Year D, 19; Year E, 13.

9. *Dividends.* Dividends have been paid on the preferred stock since its issuance. The common stock has received dividends as follows: Year A, $2.22; Year B, $1.20; Year G, $1.50; Year D, $1.20; Year E, $1.40.

10. *Depreciation.* The policy of the company is to set aside in a reserve account such amounts as will be sufficient to replace the property at the end of its useful life, estimated to be an average of twenty years. Ordinary repairs and renewals are charged to expenses. The estimated life of autos and trucks is four years. The company's depreciation policy is a straight line one.

11. *Prices.* Raw tobacco prices increased 10% in Year E. They were fairly constant in the previous years. Sales prices of the manufactured product were approximately 10% higher in Years C, D, and E, as compared with Years A and B.

Advisory 8

To Extend Credit

1. *Importance of financial statements.* A prolific source of credit information is the customer's financial report. This may consist of only the balance sheet, supplemented, as it usually is, with collateral information, or it may contain both the balance sheet and the profit and loss, or income statement.

The balance sheet shows the financial condition of a business as of a certain date. This statement indicates what the amount of the capital is, and how it is invested in the business. This throws considerable light upon the essential question, "Is the capital adequate to carry on the business as organized?" The balance sheet does not by itself create a basis of credit, but, where it appears that the applicant is entitled to it, the statement may be of substantial help in determining "how much."

In times past, some creditors were timid in asking for financial statements, because such requests were regarded by many dealers as being in the nature of a personal offense, or an unwarranted attempt to pry into their business. This viewpoint has materially changed.

The dealer knows how essential credit is to him. He also realizes that the creditors have a stake in his affairs. The issuing of a statement, therefore, is an acknowledgment of the creditor's interest, and a straightforward basis for cooperation. It not only gives the credit man a basis for judging the amount of credit to extend, but it enables him, at times, to make helpful suggestions to the debtor.

In other respects, too, the practice of issuing financial statements is beneficial to debtors. It impresses them with the importance of keeping and using business records as an aid to the planning and operating of their business. Furthermore, it has a salutary restraining influence. When a debtor knows that his financial showing will be scrutinized, he frequently avoids overextending his operations or entering upon speculative ventures.

The necessity of making financial statements is now seldom questioned by seekers of credit. In some lines, it is the custom to make such statements at fixed times and, during the intervening period, to submit trial balances to those creditors whose interest justifies it. The information contained in the balance sheet is supplemented by other data which reflects the financial, operating, and protective practices of a business. The scope of such items is being widened steadily.

2. *Practice in obtaining statements.* Most financial statements are made available to the creditor through the credit agencies. This is a valuable part of the agency's service. There are instances, however, where the statements which appear in agency reports do not satisfy the credit grantor. Sometimes, such statements are incomplete, out of date, or unsigned. Where the statement which is provided by the agency lacks sufficient detail, the creditor may prefer to have his own more carefully prepared form filled out.

This is often the case where the creditor's own form is designed to bring out information which may be especially significant in a given line of business. Where the form is properly prepared and is in sufficient detail, the experienced credit man can obtain a clear picture as to the financial condition of the business if the form is filled out in a satisfactory manner. This places him in a position to ask for more particulars in case the financial showing is below par.

The policy which is followed by creditors in securing statements is influenced by the usage in the trade. In some lines, creditors receive statements direct from the customers who frequently send the statements before receiving a request for them. In other lines, usually where the transactions run in smaller amounts, creditors obtain financial statements through the mercantile agencies.

A request for a statement is made direct, however, whenever the circumstances demand it, such as when it is found that the statement is not available through the usual channels. A request is made direct, particularly when there appears to be a break in the chain of statements from a customer who has been issuing statements at regular intervals.

When the information which is contained in commercial reports is of a conflicting or inadequate nature, the creditor may make a direct request to the customer for a recent financial statement or for a statement which shows approximately the current condition of his business. Under any circumstances, when a creditor asks for such a statement, he should do it in a tactful manner.

Some houses ask for a statement at the time of the opening of an account, while others require a statement from customers once a year. In the textile trades, the issuance of statements has assumed such large proportions that, in the interests of both the customers and the creditors, a method has been devised for centralizing this activity through the services of the National Credit Office.

3. *Laws governing the issuance of statements.* The credit man places reliance on the truthfulness of a financial statement when he uses it as a basis for measuring credit. The false statement is a treacherous weapon. It not only victimizes creditors who rely on it, but it serves to undermine the credit system. False Statement Laws have been passed, providing for the punishment of offenders.

The New York statutes in connection with false financial statements make it a crime:

a) To make a false financial statement with intent that it shall be relied upon for the purpose of procuring the delivery of personal property, etc.
b) Knowingly to procure property by the use of a false statement made by another.
c) To represent at a later date, either orally or in writing, that a statement previously made would be true on that date when, in fact, the statement then would be false, and procuring property upon the faith thereof.

Offenders, under the New York statutes, are guilty of misdemeanors, and are punishable by imprisonment of not more than one year or by a fine of not more than $1,000, or by both fine and imprisonment. The statutes of other states are somewhat similar to those of New York.

In prosecuting the maker of a false financial statement under the New York laws, it is not necessary to prove that any property was obtained upon the basis of the statement. In some states, the crime is not committed unless property has been obtained. The points of proof required may be briefly summarized. It must be established:

a) That the statement is materially false.
b) That it was made or used in order to obtain new credit or the extension of existing credit.
c) That the statement was made or used with intent that it should be relied upon.
d) That the statement was made in the county in which the maker is prosecuted.

4. *False statements through the mails.*

If a false statement upon which an extension of credit is based is sent through the mails, the offender may be prosecuted under federal statutes. In some instances, it is found desirable to prosecute in the federal courts. Sometimes, it is more convenient and easier to establish that the mails were used to defraud.

In such cases, there must not only be proof that the statement was illegal, but proof that the statement was sent through the United States mails. Consequently, it is necessary to retain envelopes in which financial statements are received, and to note on them what they contained, and when and by whom they were opened. This is simplified by using a self-mailing form of financial statement.

Another safeguard with regard to financial statements is provided in Section 442 of the Penal Code of the State of New York, which reads as follows:

Where property is purchased by aid of a duly signed financial statement, and in said statement the buyer shall state that he conducts a specified kind of business and keeps books of account of said business, upon failure to pay for such property at maturity of the account, the seller may, at any time, within ninety days thereafter, request the buyer to produce his said books of account within ten days after such request. The buyer shall then permit the seller to fully examine such books of account and to make copies of any part thereof. Failure to so produce the books is presumptive evidence that each and every pretense relating to the purchaser's means or ability to pay, in said statement contained, was false when made and known to the buyer to be false.

There is no provision in the Canadian Criminal Code similar to Section 442 of the New York State Penal Code, but the following provisions of the Canadian criminal Code may be noted here:

Section 407 (1) makes it an indictable offense falsely to pretend to enclose money in a letter. Subsection (2) of that section makes it an indictable offense, punishable by one year's imprisonment and a fine of $2,000, to make any false statement in writing respecting the financial condition or means of ability to pay of any person or corporation, for the purpose of procuring either the delivery of personal property, the payment of cash, the making of a loan or credit, the extension of a credit, the discount of an account receivable, or the making, acceptance, discount, or indorsement of a bill of exchange, check, draft or promissory note, and there is a similar provision dealing with the case where the false statement is not made by the accused, but is used by him for any of the purposes above mentioned.

Section 414 makes any promoter, director, officer, or manager of a company liable to five years' imprisonment who makes or publishes any prospectus, statement, or account which he knows to be false in any material particular, with intent to deceive or defraud shareholders or creditors, or with intent to induce any person to entrust or advance any property to such company, or to enter into any security for the benefit thereof.

Section 209 (c) states that everyone is guilty of an indictable offense who posts for transmission or delivery by or through the post any letter or circular concerning schemes devised or intended to deceive and defraud the public or for the purpose of obtaining money under false pretenses.

5. *Cooperation between the public accountant and the credit man.* There is a growing amount of cooperation between the public accountant and the credit man. This is natural, owing to their mutuality of interest. Although the accountant's loyalty is primarily to his clients, he is, along with the creditor, interested in the business man's need of accurate records and financial reports.

The credit man considers it of prime importance that his customers keep proper records as an aid in successfully conducting their business operations. In doing constructive work with the customer, the credit man needs the light thrown by financial reports upon the customer's affairs. Since the figures show the financial structure of the business, they should be complete and accurate. The statement should be not only in accordance with the books, but also with the actual condition of the business. All qualifying comments should be plainly and fully made. The value of the statement is diminished if it does not command confidence. Consequently, the accountant whose standards are high is the one who serves his clients best.

Since the accuracy of the statement in portraying the actual condition depends upon the caliber of the accountant, the credit man is much interested in the accountant's standing. If the debtor transfers his accountant from one accountant to another, the credit man is sometimes justified in inquiring into the situation for the purpose of determining its significance.

The credit man often finds it desirable to obtain from the accountant detailed information and advice as to the interpretation of items in financial statements. If the accountant cooperates, the results are beneficial to all concerned. In view of the confidential relationship between the accountant and his client, the permission of the client should be first obtained, irrespective of the circumstances.

6. *Approved forms of financial statements.* Numerous styles and forms of financial statements are in use. Those prepared and recommended by the National Association of Credit Men are used extensively. The Association also publishes a more comprehensive statement form. When folded for mailing, both these forms are self-inclosing and need no envelopes. The postmark on the statement itself is valuable evidence if it is ever necessary to prove in court that the person who made out the statement had used the mails to defraud.

In Canada, the form of financial statement required to be used is generally specified by the Companies Act under which the Company is organized.

7. *Importance of date of inventory.* Statements for credit purposes are usually prepared as of the last day of the calendar year or of a fiscal year. A fiscal year may be used either because it represents the actual anniversary of a concern, or because it lends itself to the convenience of the business. As it is natural for the financial set-up to vary from time to time, owing to seasonal and other influences, it is essential, when the items in a statement are under consideration, to keep in mind the date of the statement.

This is important in gauging the value of the items, and in judging the significance of the items in reflecting the financial strength of the concern. For example, the same amount of merchandise which would be considered normal at one time might be excessive at another. A stock of Christmas merchandise on hand October 1 might represent a very satisfactory condition, whereas it would present a different situation on December 31.

Likewise, market and price trends must be taken into account. During a period of falling prices, it is particularly important for the credit man to keep informed as to the state of the merchandise inventories of customers. The credit man must also take into consideration all developments since the date of the statement in order to reach an accurate conclusion as to the present condition of a business.

8. *Objectives of balance sheet analysis.* The credit man analyzes a financial statement primarily for the purpose of finding answers to such questions as the following:

a) What is the business man's position as to the meeting of his obligations, in other words, how liquid is his position?
b) How would his creditors fare in the event of liquidation?
c) Is he progressing? Is his sales volume going forward? Has he increased his net worth?
d) What is the trend of his financial affairs? Has his financial position become easier or more involved?
e) Is he providing adequately for replacements, depreciation, and obsolescence?
f) Does the condition of his business at the close of the year—considering the resources in which his net worth is invested—indicate that he will begin the new year under a handicap or under favorable circumstances?

To answer these questions, the credit man gives careful study to the balance sheet. He inquires into the competency and trustworthiness of the accountant who prepared the statement. The credit man realizes that the balance sheet is a summary of ledger accounts, and that it may be so drawn up as to present a wholly misleading picture. In analyzing a balance sheet, the credit man gives consideration to the various items which are discussed in the following sections.

9. *Cash.* In many statements, the item of cash is divided into two parts—cash in hand, and cash in bank. The former represents receipts not yet deposited in the bank at the time the statement was made, plus the cash kept on hand for the payment of daily operating expenses and small items. Cash in bank covers the actual bank balance as shown by the firm's check book. The total amount of cash, including both cash in hand and cash in bank, should be sufficient to meet the requirements of the business at all times.

Cash should not include I. O. U.'s, or earmarked cash which can be used only for special purposes. It should represent only such cash as is free and available for the uses of the business.

10. *Accounts receivable.* Manufacturers and wholesalers who make most of their sales on credit terms look upon their outstanding accounts as the primary source for obtaining funds. These accounts receivable should represent unpledged, outstanding accounts for merchandise sold and delivered to customers on original terms of sale.

These accounts should not include amounts owing from officers, employees, and others who are not customers. Such items should be separately stated under a heading which accurately describes what the asset represents. As a test of the quality of the accounts, it may be desirable that they be classified according to their age. In some statements, such accounts are classified as follows:

a) Not due.
b) Not more than 60 days past due.
c) More than 60 days past due.

In connection with accounts receivable, the credit man examines the statement to find out whether an adequate reserve has been set up for discounts, bad debts, returns, allowances and taxes. What this percentage should be depends upon the class of accounts carried, and upon the hazards which are peculiar to the line of business. Bad debt losses over a period of years have varied from a fraction of 1 per cent to a full 1 per cent in some lines. In other lines, bad debt losses have run up to 5 per cent. Credit policies and standards have a bearing on bad debt losses, and the credit man investigates not only the percentage of bad debts but also the quality of the customer's accounts.

Prevailing business conditions also must be taken into consideration, since, during a depression period, for instance, bad debt losses in some lines are abnormal. Nevertheless, despite any shrinkage to which accounts receivable may be subject, these accounts are a live asset to which the credit man attaches much importance.

Trade acceptances, as a balance sheet item, are considered in conjunction with the accounts receivable. The tests which apply to accounts receivable apply also to trade acceptances. Furthermore, the credit man is interested in knowing why outstanding accounts are on a trade acceptance basis. It may be due to the custom in the trade or to the usual policy of the house. It may also be due to special circumstances with which, if the amount is large enough to warrant it, the credit man should be familiar.

11. *Notes receivable.* As in the case of accounts receivable, notes receivable which are owed by customers should be stated separately from those which are owed by others. In some trades, it is the custom to make sales on a note receivable basis. Where it is the practice to sell on open account, however, the notes receivable may represent past due indebtedness or special transactions.

In such instances, if the account is of consequence, it should be investigated. Notes receivable other than those which are owed by customers, should also be investigated, particularly if they are substantial in amount, since such notes may be of doubtful value, and may point to unsound practices.

12. *Merchandise.* The item of merchandise frequently throws considerable light on the financial condition of a business. It may also be responsible for creating wrong impressions. Merchandise is an item which must be carefully interpreted. In the first place, it is important to know how the inventory was taken and whether it represents an estimate, or an actual taking of stock.

In the second place, it must be found out how the values were appraised. The merchandise should be taken at cost or at market, the lower of the two. If the market is lower than cost on the date of inventory, the difference must be treated as a loss. This means that the inventory will be taken up at replacement value, so that the concern will not be handicapped in maintaining a competitive position. On the other hand, if the market should be higher than cost, no profit will be earned until the goods are sold. Consequently, the goods should be taken up in the inventory at cost.

Where cost is the basis, the accuracy of the cost calculation or of the cost system is an important factor. As a general proposition, the goods in the inventory should be so priced that no profit is taken on goods still in stock, and these goods should be owned at prices which will permit an adequate mark-up for gross profit in fixing the selling prices. The inventory should include only such merchandise as is owned by the business, and not goods carried on consignment. If any part of the merchandise has been pledged, this fact should be stated clearly.

In evaluating the merchandise, the credit man takes into consideration the trend of prices and the nature of the goods, particularly in connection with the possibility of shrinkage in value due to physical depreciation or to a changing demand. As a help in making an analysis, the inventory is frequently segregated into three parts: raw materials, goods in process, and finished goods.

As a further help, the items of the inventory may be classified by age, and as to whether they are shopworn or defective. Out-of-style goods should be priced at their actual value.

13. *Fixed assets.* Land, buildings, machinery, and fixtures are among the fixed assets, as distinguished from the liquid assets. Each of these items should be separately stated. This will enable the credit man to form an opinion as to the value of each, the advisability of the investment, and its effect on the financial condition of the business.

Furthermore, the credit man will be in a position to judge whether an adequate reserve for depreciation with respect to each item has been set up. The credit man is also interested in knowing whether the real estate and buildings are owned for the use of the business or for investment. If they are owned for use, he considers their location and suitability for the operation of the business. If they are carried for investment, the credit man takes the trend of the market into consideration.

Where property is mortgaged, the amount of the mortgage is sometimes deducted from the value of the property and the net amount is set up as the balance sheet item. This is improper. The credit man should know both the value of the property and the amount of the mortgage, and these should be shown separately.

There have been cases where the market value of the property fell below the mortgage, because of a business recession or because a shifting of business centers caused a drop in values. In such cases, the property would in reality represent a liability. If, for instance, the property did not bring enough to satisfy the mortgage, in the event of a foreclosure, the mortgagee would have a claim against the business for the deficiency.

This matter is referred to particularly because it involves an essential principle of analysis. The credit man must know, in every instance, the gross value of an item and the amount of the encumbrance upon it, so that he can judge how adequate the margin of safety is in the light of conditions.

The fixed assets should also be considered from another angle. It is sometimes said that the fixed assets need not be considered since they cannot be used for the payment of debts. This is a superficial view. The fixed assets often give the credit man significant information. Such assets indicate the charges which will

have to be made for depreciation, and they point to funds which will be needed for the operation of the business.

Often, the fixed assets item will point strikingly to the inadequacy of the capital of a business. This item will indicate that an excessive investment has been made in such assets. With too much capital locked up in fixed assets, a strain in carrying on the business will be imposed on the remaining capital which is in liquid form. Analysis may show that the business has been organized or expanded beyond its financial strength.

14. *Organization expenses, alterations, etc.* Large outlays may be made by a concern for construction work, or for alterations on a building which the concern occupies but does not own. The entire amount of such expenses need not be charged against the business during the period when they were incurred. A reasonable charge may be made, and the balance carried forward as an asset to be written off periodically.

Sometimes, such charges are spread over the entire period of a lease. Similarly, part of the expense incurred in incorporating and in organizing a corporation may be set up as an asset to be charged off over a reasonable period. When such items appear in the balance sheet as assets, they represent part of the net worth of the business. These items should be scrutinized. There have been cases where outlays for building construction and alterations have unduly reduced the working capital and imposed a too burdensome operating charge on the business.

15. *Investments in stocks and bonds.* Usually, the credit man has two groups of securities to take into consideration. Each of these should be separately stated in the balance sheet. The first consists of stocks and bonds which are readily marketable. This item may represent a temporary investment of surplus cash, and is a quick asset. Its value is considered with reference to market prices.

The second group of securities includes the holdings of stocks and bonds in affiliated companies and in outside companies. For these securities, the market, if any, may be narrow. These types of holdings are valued in accordance with the financial condition, the earnings, and the outlook of the issuing company, and particularly with regard to their marketability.

16. *Investment in an affiliated company.* Frequently, a company will not only own the capital stock of another company, but will make advances to that company. To determine the significance of these items, it is necessary to analyze the balance sheet of the affiliated company. This will indicate the value of the capital stock and also whether the advances can be considered collectible.

Oftentimes, such advances are used by the affiliated company to cover losses, or the advances are invested in fixed assets. In fact, the condition may indicate that the affiliated company will be obliged to look to the concern for additional advances, and may become a drain on its working capital.

It is important to know whether the affiliated company is financing itself, and to what extent it may be a burden on the subject company. For the study of this situation, it is essential to have the consolidated statement of both companies or separate statements of the same date. Where the separate statements are of different dates, the intercompany transactions may be such that the statements will not show the actual financial relationship. Consequently, these statements may be misleading.

In addition to the financial relationship, answers to the following questions may be of value where there is an affiliated company:

a) What is the legal status? Has the company a controlling interest in the stock of the affiliated company?
b) What is the personal relationship? Is it friendly, and do the managements cooperate, or is there dissension?
c) What is the effect of the intercompany business transactions? Does one company trade and have other business dealings with the other, and if it does, is the relationship an advantageous one? To what extent is one dependent upon the other for sales distribution and production?

17. *Special and deferred items.* Loans receivable which are owed by partners, officers, or employees are frequently uncollectible. If the amounts are of any consequence, the credit man looks into them carefully. There have been cases in which salaries drawn by officers were not charged as an expense of the business, but were charged to the personal accounts of the officers, and were carried as an asset in order to improve a poor showing.

Overdrawn accounts or funds which are owed by salesmen are not only often uncollectible, but they may point to a weakness in the company's condition. When it appears that a concern is not operating profitably, an analysis may show that excessive, if not prohibitive, selling costs provide an explanation.

Funds appropriated for services and benefits, such as insurance, taxes, advertising, and similar items, may not be wholly used during the current year. Only such part of the appropriation as is applicable to the year is charged off; the balance is carried forward as an asset. The credit man understands the item in this light, and sometimes it may give him an inkling of the policies of the management.

18. *Liabilities.* The credit man carefully scrutinizes each liability item in order to determine the soundness of a concern's debt-paying position and its financing methods. The item of "accounts payable for merchandise" should represent the amount which a business owes on open account to trade creditors. It is important to know how much, if any, of the accounts payable are past due.

In considering "notes payable for merchandise," it should be understood whether such notes were given at the time of purchase in accordance with the usage in the trade. Unless this is the customary basis, the notes may have been given to cover past due open accounts.

A proportionate line of bank accommodation, as indicated by the notes payable to banks, is normally an element of credit strength. The credit man compares this item with the other items of indebtedness in the statement. This will frequently make clear whether the bank line is used largely to discount merchandise accounts payable, or whether the business is making full use of both mercantile and bank credit. The question arises, in some cases, as to whether a bank may not withdraw its accommodation as a result of too many renewals or for other reasons.

Because of the limited liability which attaches to stockholders of a corporation, a bank may ask, as a matter of course, for the indorsement of a corporation's note by interested individuals, without the slightest reflection upon the standing of the company. On the other hand, a bank may hold indorsements, guaranties or other security, because it does not consider that the condition of the company justifies the loan. Nevertheless, such notes represent a primary obligation of the company.

Notes and loans payable to others may include loans obtained from partners, officers, relatives, friends, or others. An item of this kind challenges the attention of the credit man. As a usual thing, a business obtains adequate credit for its normal requirements from banks and trade creditors. Should it go outside of these channels for funds, it is important to know why. There may be various explanations.

Sometimes, such an item merely represents deposits made with the business for convenience, and the amount may be such as to have no significance whatever. In some cases, funds may have been obtained in this manner as a temporary expedient, and the condition of affairs may be entirely satisfactory. In other instances, such loans may be a distinct sign of weakness.

For example, such loans may have been made because the bank line has been reduced or withdrawn. Then, again, such loans may have been necessitated because the working capital has been reduced as a consequence of losses. Another reason may be that the concern is overtrading, and cannot obtain sufficient credit for its needs from the bank and from trade creditors. At times, such loans are secured with accounts receivable or other assets pledged as collateral.

When loans are obtained from friends and relatives, particularly under forced circumstances, there is a likelihood that, in the event of impending trouble, these creditors will be paid first, to the prejudice of the interests of other creditors. As a matter of fact, such payments have been responsible for precipitating trouble.

Usually, the credit man likes to see the affairs of a concern so managed and financed that it can operate comfortably with consistent and dependable lines of bank and trade credit.

Under the head of accrued liabilities such items are included as wages, rent, and taxes, which have accrued on the date of the statement, but are not payable until the subsequent period.

Another item of liability is that of bond indebtedness. A bond usually represents a company's promise to pay funds which have been borrowed on long terms. A hand may be secured or unsecured. Very often, real or personal property may be specifically pledged as collateral for such a loan. The credit man may desire to know the nature of the debt, and what collateral underlies the bond.

Even though a bond represents an obligation which will not be due for some time, the interest, and sometimes a certain amount of amortization, is payable currently. If these payments are not met, the entire obligation on the bond may, under its terms, become immediately payable. Where the debt is a secured one, the bondholders would be entitled to the specific collateral.

If this is insufficient to discharge the obligation, they become general creditors for the unpaid balance.

19. **Real estate and chattel mortgages.** The amount a mortgage is considered in relation to the market value of the property. For instance, a mortgage is usually on a sound basis, when the borrower has a wide equity in desirable property, and has merely transformed a part of his investment in real estate into liquid assets for the proper conduct of his business. The situation is quite different, however, when the borrower has a small equity and faces the probability of a foreclosure of the mortgage, which may result in a deficiency judgment against him.

It is important to know when the mortgage is payable. In time of need, business men have borrowed on second mortgages as well as on first. Although satisfactory arrangements may have been made as to the time of payment of the first mortgage, such may not be the case with respect to the second mortgage. Consequently, it is important for the credit man to investigate all such obligations.

The chattel mortgage is a form used when the collateral underlying it is merchandise, fixtures, equipment, or other personal property. Where such a mortgage has been given, the credit man should know the circumstances. It may be that the affairs of a concern are in good order, and that the mortgage has been given in connection with a purchase of equipment, in accordance with a custom in the trade.

Under other circumstances, however, it may indicate that the concern is short of funds and is compelled to resort to this method of financing in order to obtain money. This is particularly so when it is necessary to pledge liquid assets in order to obtain funds, since, in such a case, the interests of unsecured creditors may be jeopardized. On learning that a chattel mortgage has been issued, the credit man will make it a point to ascertain just what the situation is.

20. **Reserves.** For various purposes, charges are made against income or profits, and the amounts of these charges are set up as reserves. For instance, such reserves may be established to take care of depreciation of plant, furniture and fixtures, and other such items.

The period during which such property has been used should be charged with an adequate amount for depreciation, and the same amount should be credited to a reserve account. Reserves of this kind represent an actual shrinkage in the value of the assets.

Reserves are also set up as a protection against uncertain and unknown contingencies. A concern which is engaged in a law suit will set up a reserve to discharge the liability that may arise from a verdict against it. Reserves for bad debts have already been referred to in the discussion of accounts receivable.

A reserve may be created as protection against obsolescence of equipment, or against a decline in values of securities, of merchandise, or of other property. Whether or not such reserves are adequate depends upon the circumstances surrounding the values of the assets, and upon the probability of contingencies ripening into liabilities.

21. *Surplus.*   The surplus of a business is a part of its net worth. The credit man is interested in what the surplus represents. Very often, it consists of an accumulation of net earnings. It may, however, be made up of various other items. For instance, there is the paid-in surplus. This means that the stockholders, in order to create a surplus, have paid in more than the par value of their stock. Sometimes, stockholders make donations or contributions for the benefit of the business, and these are credited to the surplus account.

The surplus may also be enhanced through the appreciation of assets. For instance, the value of a plant may be found, upon appraisal, to be higher than the amount at which it is carried on the books. In some cases of this kind, the amount which represents the difference between the appraisal and the book value is added to the asset account, and a corresponding credit is entered in the surplus account.

In some instances, although a business has actually suffered a loss as a result of its operations, it has been able to show an increase in the surplus because of an appreciation in the value of its assets, or because of income received from sources outside of the business. Such additions to the surplus account, when their nature is unknown to the credit man, may mislead him to believe that the business is a profitable one, when, as a matter of fact, such additions to the surplus are concealing losses. Dividends which have been declared or paid are charged against the surplus.

When the assets are properly valued, and there is a real surplus, it adds that much strength to the net worth. It is a particularly attractive item when it is indicative of earning power and of conservative financial management. There are situations, however, when the credit man may have some apprehension concerning the surplus account. This would be true in the case of a company which has an abnormally large surplus in relation to its capital stock, and whose entire net worth, including the surplus, is needed for the financing of the business.

The surplus may be liquidated, all, or in part, through the payment of cash dividends. An unwise distribution of the surplus could have serious consequences. Another matter to be considered is the possible influence of laws relating to taxes on the undistributed surplus of a concern. A cash dividend should be paid only to the extent warranted by the liquid strength of a business.

Advisory 9

Analysis of Financial Statements and Reports

1. *The financial strength of a business.* To conduct a business, a company has a certain amount of its own capital or net worth. Whether this capital is adequate depends not so much upon its amount as upon the way it is used in the business. The balance sheet gives an exhibit of the investment, showing the assets acquired and the liabilities incurred. The difference between the total assets, properly valued, and the total liabilities is the net worth.

It is necessary for the credit man to consider what part of this net worth is current and, therefore, available for the discharge of obligations as they mature. Such payments will ordinarily be made from those assets which are current; that is, those assets which, in the usual course of the business, can be converted into cash, or which are readily marketable. The relation of such current assets to the liabilities is considered first in determining the liquidity of the position.

In making a study of the liquid assets, the credit man considers, with respect to each item, its value, the turnover, and the conditions which will affect its being realized upon. The amount by which those assets which can be converted into cash will exceed the liabilities when they mature indicates the margin of safety in the working capital. Where this margin is substantial, the ledger experiences should show that the concern is discounting or paying promptly. Otherwise, it may be that the figures do not portray the actual condition.

Where the amount which can be counted upon for realization is less than the amount of liabilities, the concern is short of working capital. In such cases, the concern will very likely be slow pay. If it is not, it may be because it is selling assets at a sacrifice, or because it is borrowing funds—often by pledging some of its assets.

The credit man considers carefully the payment record in the light of the balance sheet. Where the situation is an inconsistent one, he inquires into the causes in order to have an accurate understanding of the actual condition. In studying the relationship of the current assets to current liabilities, the credit man also takes into account the commitments of the concern for merchandise and equipment which have not yet been delivered.

An analysis of the liquid assets in relation to the liabilities will indicate the strength of the financial position for working purposes. At this point, the credit man considers what burden must be carried by the working capital. He knows that the business will need funds to meet its liabilities and, in addition, to provide for current expenses and outlays, such as payrolls, rent, and miscellaneous running expenses. In this connection, the date of the statement is significant. The statement may show a liquid condition, and yet this may be entirely due to the favorable time at which the statement was prepared.

The credit man is concerned with how the business will be able to finance itself at the height of its operations. This is particularly true with respect to a seasonal business. Analyzing the statement with this in mind, the credit man may find it necessary to ask for data showing the concern's assets and liabilities at the peak of its operations. It is at this stage that the business is tested as to whether it has enough capital in liquid form to permit sound financing.

After satisfying himself that the working capital is adequate for all normal needs of the business, the credit man asks whether such capital will be subjected to any additional demands. Has the company any contingent liabilities? In other words, is the concern a guarantor or an endorser? Has it discounted accounts receivable or notes? Furthermore, has it any outside investments which will call for additional funds for the purpose of protection or expansion? Has it any affiliated or subsidiary companies which may require financial assistance?

In short, the credit man should find out whether or not the liquid assets are sufficient not only to take care of the liabilities but also to leave enough working capital for the financing of the business as organized, and for meeting all the other requirements of the concern.

2. *Comparative statements.* The statement of an individual concern can be interpreted more advantageously if comparison is made with previous statements. Comparative analysis will indicate certain important trends. It will show whether the firm is increasing or decreasing its capital. In either case, the financial condition may have been improved or weakened.

A concern may show an increase in net worth; yet an analysis of its statement may disclose that an undue additional amount of the capital has been invested in fixed assets. Whether too much of the capital has been invested in fixed assets, or whether there is a trend in that direction, may be disclosed by comparing the current ratios of sales to fixed assets, net worth to fixed assets, and current assets to fixed assets with ratios shown by previous statements.

A comparison of the ratios of current assets to fixed assets will indicate whether the proportion of one or the other to total assets has been increasing or decreasing. Such a comparison will show whether there has been an undue expansion of fixed assets for the purpose of increasing the volume of sales, and whether, in consequence, current assets have been reduced to an inadequate level.

Changes in the relationship of current assets to current liabilities is another important matter to consider. Even though an increase in capital is represented by liquid assets, the composition of these liquid assets may have undergone a change, and the general condition made less favorable. This might be the case where the merchandise item showed a change from a normal amount to an excessive one.

A comparative study of the assets and liabilities, from year to year, sheds light on all such changes. Even though a company is making profits, the credit man is concerned with whether it is maintaining a liquid position, and managing its affairs so as to preserve it. Since it is of paramount importance to know just how liquid a company's condition is, it is essential to know whether the trend of the company's affairs is toward greater or less liquidity.

3. *Use of ratios in analyzing statements.* The credit man wants to know the present financial condition of the credit seeker, and his business ability as shown by his management of the capital invested in the business. The credit man also wants information on the progress of the firm over a period of time long enough to furnish a sound basis of judgment. The credit man will keep in mind the specific requirements of the credit seeker's business and the characteristics of those with whom his firm is dealing.

It is helpful, in analyzing a concern's statements, to make use of various measurements which, while in no sense infallible, or necessarily adaptable to all conditions, aid the credit man in reaching a sound decision.

Important guides of this kind are the various ratios which have been worked out, some of which are discussed in the following paragraphs.

4. *Types of ratios.* Ratios are used to reflect the situation from different angles. Financial ratios show the sources, uses, and returns of the capital invested in a business. Operating ratios measure turnover, costs and profits. Dynamic ratios measure turnover. Static or balance sheet ratios show the current financial condition in different ways.

An important method of comparative check on the progress of the credit seeker is an analysis of the business over a period of years, at least five. This, when presented in ratio form, is sometimes referred to as a horizontal ratio.

5. *Current position-quick ratios and current ratios.* A ratio of 100 per cent is taken as the minimum of safety as between liquid assets (cash, marketable securities, notes and accounts receivable, less proper reserves) and current liabilities which include notes and accounts payable, and adequate reserve for taxes. Although a ratio of 2 to 1 (current assets twice current liabilities), is usually assumed as orthodox, this is subject to variation in particular cases. A definite knowledge of operating conditions in the business is necessary not only to fix a standard for each ratio but also to interpret fluctuations resulting from cyclical and seasonal factors.

More satisfactory tests of current position are cash to notes payable (indicating the degree of bank sponsorship since banks commonly require a 20 per cent deposit margin on loans) and the quick or liquid ratio. When expanding under favorable business conditions, the surplus policy should be such that a substantial portion of earnings is retained to finance the expenses. From the current tax standpoint, however, surplus reserves should not be maintained at excessive levels as this may increase the tax burden on the retained earnings.

6. *Operating ratios.* The two chief indicators of stress and strain from overtrading and overborrowing are declining relations of sales to net worth, and of sales to working capital. The ratios which measure the efficient use of available funds are as follows:

   a. The average age of receivables.
   b. The average age of inventory.
   c. The average age of conversion.
   d. The average age of current liabilities.
   e. The average age of working capital.

To find the average age of receivables, divide receivables by sales and multiply by 365. To find the average age of inventory, divide inventory by sales and multiply by 365. To find the average age of conversion, take the sum of the average age of receivables and the average age of inventory. This will represent the average age of conversion in days; namely, the time necessary to complete the cycle from cash to inventory to receivables and to cash again.

To find the average age of current liabilities, divide them by sales and multiply by 365. To find the average age of working capital, subtract the average age of current liabilities from the average age of conversion. The rate of turnover of any of these ratios, measured in days, is found by dividing the number of days by 365.

7. *Other useful ratios.* The relation between inventory and working capital is important. It has been stated that a company, which has a net worth of less than $250,000, cannot, with safety, invest more than 67 per cent of its working capital in inventory. On the other hand, a firm, which has a net worth of $250,000 or over, may have as much as 75 per cent of its working capital so invested. Similar percentages are suggested as safe relations between net fixed assets and tangible net worth.

Various other tests have been devised of more or less general application, depending on special trade conditions and the general business situation. A valuable ratio, which has to do with fixed assets and funded debt, is that between total debt and tangible net worth. This must, of necessity, be less than 100 per cent. It is believed that the permissible limit would not exceed 95 per cent.

It is said that not over 75 per cent of tangible net worth should be invested in fixed assets. It is possible to do a larger volume of business on the working capital than safety would justify, and this is sometimes done by a firm which is sound. Nevertheless, a company doing this frequently under normal business conditions would be in trouble if its expectations as to conditions should not be realized.

A suggested maximum volume of sales is the lower of two results arrived at separately. Divide 365 by the average age of the working capital and multiply by 90 per cent of the working capital. Compare the result with that secured by dividing 365 by the average age of the inventory and multiplying by 75 per cent of the working capital. The lower of the two is taken because, if the turnover of the working capital is too rapid, too much of it is tied up in inventory to permit the company to meet current obligations properly.

8. *Horizontal ratios and median studies.* Robert Morris Associates, an organization of bank credit men, has collected data from the basic industries to show typical ratios and variations. Mr. Alexander Wall, Secretary Treasurer, took a large number of statements from several lines of business and studied their characteristics. From these, he evolved a typical statement for each line, expressed in the form of a ratio. Further studies, resulting in the development of important median ratios, have been made by Mr. Roy A. Foulke, Vice-President of Dun and Bradstreet, Inc. Such activities help to set standards of accomplishment for particular concerns.

9. *Current assets to current liabilities.* We have already pointed out that the determination of a concern's ability to discharge its obligations involves first a study of its current assets in relation to its current liabilities. Current assets include cash, accounts receivable, merchandise, marketable securities, and such other item as can be currently realized upon.

Current liabilities are obligations which are due, or will become due, currently or within a year. They include such items as the following: indebtedness on open account for merchandise, whether or not due; notes payable for merchandise; notes payable to banks; notes payable to others, secured or unsecured; and miscellaneous accounts payable.

In fact, current liabilities include all debts except those covered by long-term obligations, such as bond issues, long term notes, etc. As has been previously observed, however, the current interest charges which accrue on long-term liabilities, and the amounts required for current amortization represent current liabilities.

It is the proceeds of the current assets which give a concern the funds with which to pay its debts and to meet its running expenses. The excess of such current assets over liabilities represents the working capital of the business. The old rule that current assets should be double current liabilities is not an entirely dependable guide. In certain lines, it may be necessary for the ratio to be considerably more than double. In other instances, there is a possibility that it can be less.

In order to form an opinion as to the adequacy of the working capital, it is often necessary to consider individually all of the assets and the liabilities. The following points should be considered:

a. AS TO AN ASSET:
    1. What is its value?
    2. When will it be realized upon?
    3. Is it in proper proportion to the other assets, to the sales, working capital, and net worth?
    4. What is the outlook as to gain or shrinkage in the course of liquidating it?
    5. Is it padded, and does it present a misleading view of the condition?

b. AS TO A LIABILITY:
    1. When is it payable?
    2. Is it in accordance with the financial strength of the business, or does it indicate overextension, or a tendency in that direction?
    3. Does it reflect any weakness in the financial structure?

10. *Cash to notes payable to banks.* It is usually understood that a borrower will carry a balance equal to at least 20 per cent of his indebtedness at the banks. The comparison of these two items will, therefore, be helpful in making a study of the cash position. The amount of cash is also to be considered in relation to the size and needs of the business.

11. *Sales to accounts receivable.* This comparison shows the turnover of the accounts receivable, and throws light on the collectability of the accounts. As a starting point, in making

this test, let us take a hypothetical case and ascertain what the average of accounts receivable should be on the basis of certain specified sales and terms.

If, for instance, sales for the year are $1,200,000,000 on 60-day terms, the average figure for accounts receivable would be one-sixth of $1,200,000 or $200,000. This would represent average shipments for 60 days. In other words, the accounts receivable would be turned over, on the average, six times.

If, however, the actual accounts receivable item in the balance sheet were $300,000, the amount would be far in excess of the average. It would represent one quarter of the year's sales, or average shipments for 90 days. This would be a turnover of four times. This excess of accounts receivable above the $200,000 average could be accounted for by one or more of the following:

a) Shipments during the last 60 days, because of seasonal or other influences, might have been in excess of the average shipments for 60 days during the year.

b) The accounts receivable might have included past due accounts.

c) They might have improperly included advances or loans to affiliated companies, deficits of salesmen, loans to officers, and other items which did not represent accounts receivable from customers.

d) The accounts receivable might have included sales made on installment terms.

If, on the other hand, the actual accounts receivable were $100,000, the turnover would be twelve times. The accounts receivable would thus represent one-twelfth of the year's sales, or average shipments for 30 days. Accounts receivable $100,000 below the $200,000 average could be accounted for by one or more of the following:

a) Shipments during the 60 days prior to statement date might have been because of seasonal or other reasons, below the average shipments for 60 days during the year.

b) Shipments during the period might have been paid in anticipation prior to their due dates.

c) Substantial shipments might have been made on a cash basis.

d) Accounts might have been sold or might have been pledged as collateral for loans.

12. *Sales to merchandise.* The merchandise turnover can be ascertained by dividing the merchandise item into the sales. If exactness is required, the stocks of merchandise at cost should be divided into the cost of the merchandise sold in order to show how many times the merchandise has been turned into sales. It usually serves the purposes of analysis, however, to compare the sales at selling prices with the merchandise as stated in the balance sheet.

The importance of this question of turnover cannot be overemphasized. The credit man keeps well posted as to the rate of turnover in the lines of trade in which he is interested. If the turnover in a particular case is slow, it may indicate that the stock contains merchandise which is stale, shopworn, out of style, or, for other reasons, unsalable. An excessive supply of merchandise often handicaps the sales efforts, and frequently leads to unprofitable sales. Slow-moving stock is a common cause of slow payments.

On the other hand, a supply of merchandise beyond the normal amount may reflect good judgment on the part of the management in taking advantage of favorable market conditions, or in assuring itself of an adequate supply in periods of shortages and extraordinary demands. Such practices, however, should be appraised from the standpoint of market conditions and the financial status of the concern.

The salability of the merchandise and its realizable value are of prime importance. The credit man, in the course of cooperating with his customers, frequently analyzes the stock on hand so as to form an opinion as to its value, the hazards to which it is subject, and the possibilities of turning it into profitable sales.

The rate of turnover varies with the line of business. Perishable goods, which are purchased for immediate resale, have a more rapid turnover than goods which are manufactured by slow processes, or finished goods which are carried for shipment at seasonal periods.

It is not unusual for concerns which are unable to pay their bills promptly to have an excessive investment in merchandise. For example, a small dealer who does a business of $24,000 a year might show, in his statement, merchandise at cost of $8,000. This would represent a turnover of three times, or a stock on hand equal to over five months' average sales at selling prices.

13. *Receivables to merchandise.* The statements for two successive years may show exactly the same amount of total current assets to total current liabilities. Although the ratio remains unchanged, yet the financial position may be quite different. This may be due to a change in the proportions of the accounts and merchandise which enter into the total current assets.

Thus, in determining as to whether there is too much dependence on credit, it is necessary to do more than give consideration to the relationship of total current assets to total current liabilities in determining the position of the concern with regard to meeting liabilities when they mature. In addition, the ratio of current assets, exclusive of merchandise, to liabilities should be considered. Are these quick assets sufficient for the discharge of obligations? If not, will the required additional amount be realized in time from the sale of merchandise?

Other tests are made for the purpose of determining the adequacy of the working capital. Certain of these tests serve to show whether there is under trading or overtrading from the standpoint of the amount of working capital. Under trading may result in losses. In the case of overtrading, on the other hand, the working capital may become too frail a support for the concern's financial structure. If the margin of working capital becomes narrower when operations are expanding, it is obvious that the risk increases.

In making tests which bear on this matter, it is necessary to have an understanding as to what the normal or average turnover is under comparable conditions. In other words, the credit man must be familiar with such turnovers in a similar line of business.

14. *Sales to not worth.* The ratio of sales to net worth shows how many times the net worth is turned into sales. A large turnover may indicate that the business is being efficiently and profitably conducted. On the other hand, it may give rise to the question as to whether the concern is attempting to do too much business or, in other words, whether it is undercapitalized. This requires a study of the relation of "the net worth to the labilities," in order to determine whether too much credit is being used in proportion to the net worth.

A further test as to the liquidity of a business is found in the ratio of "net worth to fixed assets." Is too much of a firm's capital locked up in fixed assets? In view of the volume of business which is being done, will the financial requirements for operating the plant impose a strain upon the working capital? Where there appears to be overtrading, it is also well to consider the relation of "sales to net profits." A large business may be done on a very small margin of profit. Under such circumstances, a considerable amount of risk is involved, particularly if the business is organized so as to be dependent upon a large volume.

If the study of relationships indicates, however, that there is under trading, this may mean that sales are not covering the expenses of the business, and that, consequently, the business is operating at a loss.

15. *Front and loss or income statement.* Liquid assets may be increased by profits or shrunk by losses. Light on these possibilities is found in an examination of the profit and loss statement. Some of the items which are usually significant in the study of a profit and loss statement are as follows:

a) Sales.
b) Returns.
c) Gross profits.
d) Depreciation.
e) Selling expenses.
f) Bad debts.
g) Rent.
h) Officers' salaries, administrative and general expenses.
i) Net profits.

SALES. It is the purpose of a business to make a profit on its sales. It may be found that a business is overtrading from the standpoint of the amount of working capital. This may be due to the carrying of excessive merchandise inventories or outstanding accounts. It may also be due to the fact that too much capital has been locked up in fixed assets. The investment in fixed assets, while increasing the facilities for larger business, may reduce the amount of liquid capital with which to conduct it.

Sales, therefore, are compared with the net worth, with the various current assets, and with the fixed assets. The comparison of sales with fixed assets may point to a too heavy investment in plant. On the other hand, such a comparison may show an inadequate volume of sales as the result of under trading. In the latter case, losses may be indicated as a consequence of inactive assets and idle equipment.

RETURNS. In some profit and loss statements, the sales are shown net, or, in other words, the amount of gross sales minus the amount of merchandise returned. This is unsatisfactory to the credit man. The, gross sales and the amount of returned merchandise should be shown separately. In some industries, returned merchandise constitutes a very appreciable item. It either indicates poor standards in the trade, or inefficient manufacturing or merchandising on the part of the concern.

GROSS PROFITS. The difference between income from net sales and the costs of goods is gross profit. It is essential to know how the gross profit of a given concern compares with similar earnings of successful concerns in the industry. The gross profit may be the key to the study of the efficiency of the management.

A relatively small gross profit may be traced to the fixing of selling prices at an incorrect level, to high costs, to inventory losses, or to a combination of the three. When there is inefficiency in purchasing or in production, a concern will have higher costs and, consequently, a smaller gross profit than a more efficient competitor, after allowing for any difference in the size of the two concerns.

Assuming, however, that costs are at the most economical level possible, selling prices may be too low. This may be due either to poor sales management or to competitive conditions in the industry. In times of depression and reduced production, however, when prices are declining, and there is an increase in the percentage of overhead expense, the gross profits of a concern may suffer not only from too low prices but also from high costs through no fault of the management.

On the other hand, in the case of an expanding market in a period of good times, rising prices without a corresponding increase in costs will feature the situation. In such a period, gross profits of a concern may improve regardless of inefficiency on the part of the management.

It is thus important for the credit man to compare the gross profit of a particular concern with that of other concerns of the same size in the industry. The credit man can, in this way, test the management and come to an understanding as to the strength of the concern under consideration.

DEPRECIATION. The financial result is not accepted by the credit man until he is satisfied that ample reserves have been provided for all necessary purposes and contingencies.

SELLING EXPENSES. In fixing its selling prices, a concern allows a certain percentage on the sales to cover selling expenses. A test of the selling expense is to compare it with the sales. Such a test may show that the selling expense is excessive. The unfavorable result may be due to temporary conditions, to unfavorable competition, or to the inefficiency of the salesmen.

Sometimes, however, it may be due to new methods of distribution. An analysis of the item may show that excessive cost is inherent in the situation, or that it applies only to certain territories, and may or may not be subject to correction. The importance of this item varies with different lines of trade, and, in some lines, it is a very serious matter.

BAD DEBTS. A calculation is made to determine the percentage of bad debts in relation to sales. The losses are considered in the light of the circumstances, and often provide an indication as to whether or not the policies of the credit and sales departments are sound.

RENT. In the case of many concerns, rent is an important item. It is an overhead expense and must be justified by a sufficient volume of profitable business. Very often, a dealer will undertake to pay more rent than he can afford. To do the volume necessary to war rant this overhead expense, he is obliged to extend his operations, and thereby to incur liabilities which will impose a strain upon his working capital.

OFFICERS, SALARIES, ADMINISTRATIVE AND GENERAL EXPENSES. Officers should draw a reasonable compensation for their services. Their salaries, like the wages of employees, should be limited by the amounts which the business can properly afford to pay for the value received. Extravagant salaries tend to make questionable the sense of responsibility of the officers. Similarly, all other administrative and general expenses should be in accordance with the sound needs of the business.

NET PROFITS. The continuance of a concern as a going business depends upon its profitableness. Does the business yield a reasonable return on the capital invested? What is the relation of "net profits to net worth"? How do the earnings compare with net profits of other concerns conducting comparable businesses? what percentage are earnings of sales?

When the margin is a very thin one, it is important to keep this in mind in considering the other items of the profit and loss statement, such as gross profit and selling expenses, in order to form an opinion as to the adequacy of the margin of safety represented by the percentage of net profit.